HOME OFFICE RESEARCH STUI

Case Screening by The Crown Prosecution Service: How And Why Cases Are Terminated

by Debbie Crisp and David Moxon

A HOME OFFICE
RESEARCH AND PLANNING UNIT
REPORT

LONDON: HMSO

© *Crown copyright 1994*
Applications for reproduction should be made to HMSO
Printed in the United Kingdom for HMSO
Dd. 300311 C10 12/94

ISBN 0 11 341137 5

HOME OFFICE RESEARCH STUDIES

'Home Office Research Studies' comprise reports on research undertaken in the Home Office to assist in the exercise of its administrative functions, and for the information of the judicature, the services for which the Home Secretary has responsibility (direct or indirect) and the general public.

On the last pages of this report are listed titles already published in this series, in the preceding series *Studies in the Causes of Delinquency and the Treatment of Offenders,* and in the series of *Research and Planning Unit Papers.*

HMSO

Standing order service

Placing an order with HMSO BOOKS enables a customer to receive other titles in this series automatically as published.

This saves time, trouble and expense of placing individual orders and avoids the problem of knowing when to do so.

For details please write to HMSO BOOKS (PC11B.2), Publications Centre, P.O. Box 276, London SW8 5DT and quoting reference 25.08.011.

The standing order service also enables customers to receive automatically as published all material of their choice which additionally saves extensive catalogue research. The scope and selectivity of the service has been extended by new techniques, and there are more than 3,500 classifications to choose from. A special leaflet describing the service in more detail may be obtained on request.

Foreword

Ever since the Crown Prosecution Service was set up in 1986 there has been controversy over the exercise of its powers to discontinue cases. Early criticism that the new service too readily took its lead from initial police decisions have been replaced by criticisms that it too often rejects cases submitted by the police. There has hitherto been little detailed information about the process whereby cases are terminated to assess such claims. This report presents the findings of a study which looked in detail at the reasons why the CPS discontinues cases, and at the way the police and prosecutors interact in bringing cases to a conclusion. An interim report was prepared for the Royal Commission on Criminal Justice.

The study involved collaboration with the CPS, whose cooperation in providing data and participating in interviews was essential to the project.

ROGER TARLING
Head of Research and Planning Unit

Acknowledgements

The wholehearted cooperation of the Crown Prosecution Service, at both national and local level, was essential to the project. We are indebted to all members of the CPS who assisted with the development of the project, the many who completed forms for the main project and those who participated in interviews. We are also grateful to the police officers who agreed to be interviewed.

Home Office colleagues, notably Julie Vennard and David Brown, who gave much support and assistance in setting up the project, and Jessica Harris, Anna Meadow, Viki D'Amore and Claire Whittaker who helped with the analysis.

DEBBIE CRISP
DAVID MOXON

Contents

Foreword		iii
Acknowledgements		iv
Summary		vi
Chapter 1	Introduction	1
Chapter 2	Overview	7
Chapter 3	**Reasons for termination**	15
Chapter 4	**Consultation between the police and CPS**	27
Chapter 5	**Timing and notification of decisions to terminate**	33
Chapter 6	**Discussion**	37
Appendix A	Sample breakdown by area	43
Appendix B	Area breakdown of reasons for termination for non-motoring offences	45
Appendix C	Rate of termination by offence group	47
References		49
Publications		51

Summary

This study reports the main findings of research on termination of cases by the Crown Prosecution Service.

The CPS was set up in 1986, in response to a recommendation of the Royal Commission on Criminal Procedure which reported in 1981 The Royal Commission was concerned about the inefficiency, lack of openness and inconsistency of the procedures then in place, and the central purpose in setting up the CPS was to provide independent scrutiny of cases instituted by the police, and to assess whether the strength of the evidence and public interest considerations made prosecution appropriate. There has been particular interest in the way the CPS exercises its powers to terminate cases submitted by the police.

In order to evaluate the screening of cases by the CPS the study obtained samples of 1,286 terminated cases and 2,201 cases which proceeded to court. In addition, there were 443 cases involving advice files only, whereby the police approach the CPS for formal advice about whether the case should be pursued. The data from these sources were supplemented by interviews with crown prosecutors and police officers to provide a better understanding of the processes underlying the statistical findings.

Thirteen CPS branches from seven areas participated in the study. The branches were selected to provide a wide range of characteristics as regards termination rates and numbers of advice files submitted by the police, and to provide a mix of rural and urban areas.

Main findings

Termination rates in the 13 branches ranged from 10 per cent to 20 per cent.

Termination on evidential grounds

Among cases which were terminated, 58 per cent of non-motoring and 47 per cent of motoring cases were dropped on evidential as opposed to public interest grounds. As compared with cases proceeding to court, those terminated on evidential grounds tended to have fewer evidential factors on file, and in particular were less likely to include eye-witness evidence or a confession or admission. When motoring cases were excluded, the most common reasons for termination on evidential grounds were:

- lack of supporting or corroborative evidence, which featured in 39 per cent of terminations;
- anticipated problems with witnesses (in terms of reliability, availability or willingness to give evidence) which were a factor in 35 per cent of terminations;

SUMMARY

- insufficient evidence of a key element of the offence was cited in 19 per cent of terminated cases.

Other evidential weaknesses, conflict between witnesses, the strength of the defence or the inadmissibility of evidence each featured in about 5 per cent of cases.

Termination on public interest grounds

Among terminated cases, 35 per cent of non-motoring and 24 per cent of motoring cases were dropped on public interest grounds. The main factors in these terminations were as follows:

- there were other files outstanding or the defendant was in custody on other matters in 38 per cent of cases;
- a nominal penalty was thought likely if the case went to court in 27 per cent of cases;
- in 21 per cent of cases the complainant did not wish to proceed;
- the triviality of the offence was mentioned in 14 per cent of terminated cases.

Less frequently mentioned factors included the youth of the defendant, the fact that the offence was stale or that the defendant was mentally ill or suffering acute stress, each mentioned in about 10 per cent of cases. Other reasons included the fact that the defendant was felt to have suffered enough, that recompense had been made to the victim or that it was a suitable case for a caution.

Other grounds for termination

Much the most common reason for dropping cases other than on evidential or public interest grounds was that it proved impossible to trace the defendant. This was common in motoring cases, where it accounted for 24 per cent of terminations, but rare for non-motoring cases where it accounted for only 3 per cent of terminations. Refusal by the court to accede to a prosecution request for adjournment accounted for 3 per cent of terminations.

Defendant characteristics

There were no significant differences beween cases terminated and those which proceeded to court in terms of the age or sex of the accused, or whether they had previous convictions. However, cases in the terminated sample were more likely to involve a family dispute, reflecting the reluctance of the complainant to give evidence in some instances and particularly where reconciliation had been achieved or was being attempted.

Offence characteristics

The seriousness of the offence strongly influenced the extent to which offences were terminated on evidential as opposed to public interest grounds. This simply reflects the fact that the more serious the case, the less likely it is that it will be appropriate to drop it on public interest grounds. Thus 81 per cent of indictable offences, around 65 per cent of either way offences (except shoplifting) but only 43 per cent of summary offences that were dropped were terminated because of evidential weaknesses. (The proportion of shoplifting cases terminated on evidential as opposed to public interest grounds was similar to the proportion for summary offences.) The findings demonstrate that the CPS is less likely to drop more serious cases on public interest grounds, which is consistent with the fact that a nominal penalty is a much less likely court outcome.

Consultation between the police and CPS

Interviews with police officers and crown prosecutors confirmed that the police were sometimes unhappy about termination of cases they felt were strong enough to succeed in court. The CPS, for their part, sometimes felt that more could have been done by the police to meet their requests for additional information. In general, communication between the CPS and the police Administrative Support Units appeared to be satisfactory. However, reasons for dropping cases did not always filter through to the officers most directly concerned with the case, which could leave them uneasy about decisions and undermine morale.

Advice file cases

In advice file cases, advice was often sought on more than one aspect of the case. The main reason for the police seeking advice (given in 83 per cent of cases) was for an assessment of the sufficiency of the evidence. Advice about the number or type of charges featured in 39 per cent and the police sought advice on whether a caution would be appropriate in 15 per cent. In only 4 per cent of cases did the police seek advice on whether it would be in the public interest to proceed. In 41 per cent of cases the CPS recommended no further action and in 44 per cent they recommended proceeding on some or all offences. There was wide variation in the use of advice files in different areas - ranging from 0.7 per cent to 13.9 per cent of cases finalised - and there was some limited evidence that branches with more advice file cases had lower termination rates.

Timing of termination

Only 5 per cent of terminated cases were dropped before the first court appearance, and a further 7 per cent at the first court appearance. In 95 per cent of cases, therefore, there was at least one court appearance. In more than one-third of terminated cases (37 per cent) the defendant had no advance notification (and in some other cases less than 48 hours notice was given). Reasons for late notification were that there was insufficient time, typically because police files were sent less than 10 days before the hearing date. However, in 29 per cent of cases where no advance notice was given this was because the defendant's whereabouts were unknown. In some cases the decision was only made at court, for example because witnesses failed to turn up.

1 Introduction

Background

The Crown Prosecution Service (CPS) was brought into being by the Prosecution of Offences Act 1985 and became operational in 1986. The new service was set up in response to recommendations made by the Royal Commission on Criminal Procedure (1981) whose review of the existing prosecutorial system highlighted a number of deficiencies which, according to the Commission, called for a "complete reformulation and restatement of the procedure for bringing a person before the court".

Prior to the Prosecution of Offences Act each police force had its own arrangements for the prosecution of offenders, and the Commission identified wide geographical variation in prosecution policy and practice. The Commission also concluded that a high proportion of cases were being brought before the court which ought to have been filtered out at an earlier stage. For example, they pointed out that in 1978, 43 per cent of Crown Court acquittals occurred "...because the prosecution is unable to adduce sufficient evidence even to make a prima facie case". (Para 6.18.) In creating the CPS the new Act transferred the prosecution function from the police to an independent body of legally trained persons headed by the Director of Public Prosecutions. It was intended that this would lead to a more effective filtering of cases so that only appropriate cases reached court. It was also hoped that the existence of a national service would help to overcome any arbitrary variation in the treatment of cases in different areas.

The prosecution process starts with the police, and may be instigated by means of a charge or a summons (whereby a letter is sent to the defendant calling them to appear before the court). The principles upon which the Crown Prosecution Service exercises its functions are set out in the Code for Crown Prosecutors. The Code is a public document which is regularly updated, and is laid annually before Parliament as part of the CPS Annual Report. Since the research was completed the Code has undergone substantial revision (CPS 1994). The basic principles are the same, but efforts have been made to clarify the Code and to "bring out the factors in favour of a prosecution more clearly" (CPS 1994). The changes, therefore, will tend to strengthen the presumption in favour of prosecution, and it is hoped that greater clarity will make for greater consistency. The central aim of the Code has always been to promote efficiency and consistency in decision-making throughout the country, with the aid of a two-tiered test by which all cases must be assessed prior to prosecution.

The evidential test requires the prosecutor to decide whether there is enough evidence against the defendant for there to be a realistic prospect of conviction. The evidence must establish all elements of the offence, and must identify the defendant as its perpetrator. Fresh information may emerge as a case proceeds which casts doubt on the initial decision to prosecute, and cases are kept under continual review.

If the prosecutor feels that the evidence against the defendant is strong enough a second test is applied, which is whether prosecution is in the public interest. The Code sets out factors to be considered to help with this assessment, which include the personal circumstances of the defendant, the views of the victim and the level of penalty likely to be imposed by the court.

Where a prosecutor feels that the criteria set out in the Code have not been met, section 23 of the Prosecution of Offences Act empowers them to drop the case. Appropriate termination of cases by the CPS may be viewed as a "measure of the benefit of bringing an independent, legal mind to bear on the initial police decision to institute proceedings" (Gandy, 1992). When the decision has been made not to proceed with a case, the CPS can:

i) discontinue proceedings using the procedure under section 23(3) of the Prosecution of Offences Act 1985, which empowers the CPS to discontinue a case during the early stages (i.e. before evidence has been presented at a summary trial or before committal to the Crown Court);

ii) offer no evidence in court;

iii) apply to withdraw proceedings.

For the purposes of this report the expression 'termination' covers cases falling into each of these categories.

The CPS may discontinue cases under section 23(3) without reference to the court and there is no bar to the charges being re-instituted at a later stage, for example if new evidence comes to light. Where the prosecution wishes to offer no evidence in summary proceedings it must do so before the close of the prosecution case. The defendant is then viewed as acquitted and no further proceedings are permissible. Once the prosecution case has been concluded at a magistrates' court, or after a case has been committed to the Crown Court, the prosecution can only withdraw from the case with the leave of the court.

Since the inception of the CPS the rate at which cases are terminated has increased substantially. CPS statistics showed that the proportion of cases terminated increased fairly steadily from 7.7 per cent in 1987 to 13.2 per cent of the magistrates' court cases finalised nationally in 1992.[1] From CPS quarterly data, the termination rate peaked at 14.0 per cent in the last quarter of 1992 but fell back to 13.0 per cent by the third quarter of 1993. Although the increase in the proportion of cases dropped by the CPS has attracted criticism, the decision to terminate does not take place in a vacuum: it is but

---

[1] There are large differences in termination rates derived from CPS and Home Office statistics (the latter are higher) although both show a steady increase in the proportion of terminated cases. Part of the explanation for the difference is that the Home Office figures include cases adjourned *sine die*, cases discharged at committal and cases withdrawn after evidence has been offered in addition to the CPS termination categories listed. Home Office figures may also record a case as discontinued where, in fact, charges are amended and the case proceeds.

INTRODUCTION

one aspect of a process which involves a number of agencies, and is influenced by the kinds of cases drawn into that process. For example, changes in cautioning, sentencing patterns and offence patterns are all liable to affect termination rates, and in the years since the CPS was set up there has been a sharp rise in the number of offenders cautioned as a proportion of those cautioned or proceeded against, and in the use of discharges by the courts. The CPS's own concern with understanding how the filtering process is operating is reflected in monitoring which covered all cases which it discontinued in November 1993 (CPS 1994a).

Hitherto, there has been little hard information as to why the CPS terminates cases and the way in which CPS practices interact with police decision-making about whether to charge, caution or take no further action against suspects. One study, by McConville, Sanders and Leng (1991), did look at the way police officers and prosecutors reached their decisions in criminal cases, and the authors concluded that the CPS sometimes pursued evidentially weak cases "where to do so serves some police imperative". It was also claimed that the CPS often felt that the public interest was best served by uncritical acceptance of police decisions to charge. However, this study was based on a small sample of cases dealt with in 1986-88, the period just after the introduction of the CPS, when terminations were less common. In view of recent police (and public) concerns about the CPS's readiness to discontinue cases, it is worth recalling that criticism was originally levelled at the CPS for being insufficiently critical of police decisions.

Aims of the study

For the present study the Home Office Research and Planning Unit (RPU) examined the process by which the CPS decide whether to prosecute. The central aims of the RPU research were to examine:

- the kinds of cases resulting in termination and possible reasons for variations in the proportion of cases dropped in different areas;
- the specific criteria which lead to cases being dropped;
- the consultation process between crown prosecutors and supervising police officers when considering whether to discontinue, and the extent and nature of any disagreement between the police and CPS on termination;
- the types of case in which the police seek advice from the CPS prior to charge, the nature of the advice sought and the response to the advice offered;
- the stage at which cases are terminated and, where relevant, the reasons for terminating a case only after court proceedings are underway.

HOME OFFICE RESEARCH STUDY No. 137

Methodology

Selection of areas

The study was developed in close consultation with CPS Headquarters, following extensive pilot work.

In order to get some indication of the extent of and reasons for variation in termination rates, 13 CPS branches from seven different areas were selected for inclusion in the study. The areas were: Lancashire and Cumbria; London South and Surrey; Merseyside; Nottinghamshire; South Wales and Gwent; Thames Valley; and West Yorkshire. Two branches were included in all but one of these areas. This selection provided a mix of urban and rural areas, and wide variation in termination and advice rates, and in local cautioning rates. (The data collection was completed before the number of CPS areas was reduced from 31 to 13.)

Selection of sample

In order to ensure that there were enough terminated cases for detailed analyses of prosecutors' decisions not to proceed, a target of 100 cases where the CPS dropped all charges against the defendant was set for each of the 13 branches. A form was completed for each of the first 100 cases terminated prior to or at a magistrates' court from 1 October 1991. Crown Court cases were not included, as it would have been difficult to obtain big enough samples within a reasonable period, although the sample did include cases which were originally destined for the Crown Court but were dropped before committal proceedings took place. Only one branch achieved substantially less than the target sample and most areas obtained sufficient cases within the month. The forms covered information about the defendant including age, sex, employment status and criminal history, together with basic offence details and the nature of the evidence. They also charted the various stages of decision-making in relation to the case and reasons for termination.

In order to ensure a reasonable spread amongst other offence types, a ceiling of 30 per cent was placed on the proportion of motoring offences in the sample. The offence breakdown of the sample as a whole is not, therefore, necessarily representative of the overall caseload of each branch. Where there was more than one offence, the case has been categorised according to the most serious. A typical example is that a case involving taking a vehicle without the owner's consent and driving without insurance would be categorised according to the former (which is a sub-category of theft) rather than the summary offence of having no insurance.

Each branch completed another set of questionnaires which provided information about the first 170 cases which proceeded to court during the data collection period. (This sample was broken down into quotas of guilty and not guilty pleas etc., again with a 30 per cent ceiling on the proportion of motoring cases). This information provided a

INTRODUCTION

sample of cases which could be used to establish what factors distinguished cases terminated by the CPS from those which it was decided to prosecute.

Crown prosecutors completed questionnaires for all cases where the police sent a set of papers to the CPS with a request for formal pre-process advice during the month of October 1991. (A ceiling of 75 cases was set in respect of two areas with exceptionally high advice file rates, but no offence quotas were set.)

Sample sizes for each area are shown in Appendix A. The data provided by these cases were supplemented by semi-structured interviews with various different grades of both local prosecutors and police officers in the each of the areas studied. Thirty-seven crown prosecutors and 31 police officers, spread fairly evenly between areas, were interviewed about consultations on issues relating to prosecution decisions.

Structure of the report

Chapter 2 provides an overview of the samples of cases terminated and those going to court, and of variations between branches. Chapter 3 looks at the reasons why cases in the samples drawn from CPS branches were terminated. Chapter 4 looks in more detail at the consultation process between them, and Chapter 5 looks at the timing of decisions and reasons why cases are often dropped at a late stage. The issues raised by the report are discussed in Chapter 6.

HOME OFFICE RESEARCH STUDY No. 137

2 Overview

This chapter provides an overview of termination rates and other aspects of caseloads in the CPS branches which participated in the study, and compares the characteristics of cases terminated with those which proceeded to court.

Caseloads

Table 1 shows the overall throughput of cases in each of the CPS branches for the fourth quarter of 1991 (which includes the period of data collection) together with numbers of cases terminated and numbers involving advice files only.

Table 1
Overview of caseloads and advice, termination, cautioning and conviction rates for the quarter October to December 1991 for participating CPS branches[1]

Branch	Cautioning rate[2] %	Cases finalised	Advice rate %	Termination rate
A	37	1,173	2.0	14
B	4	3,793	0.7	20
C	17	2,802	5.6	15
D	17	3,771	2.7	18
E	21	786	1.5	10
F	21	6,796	0.8	12
G	13	3,189	3.0	11
H	13	3,249	3.7	11
I	10	7,083	8.0	16
J	10	5,741	13.9	10
K	12	7,812	1.7	12
L	11	5,438	2.2	15
M	11	3,538	4.5	11
England & Wales	18	382,014	4.3	11

Notes:
1 The figures (except cautioning rates) are taken from branch and national performance indicators collected by the CPS for the quarter October to December 1991. Termination and advice rates are expressed as proportions of cases finalised.
2 Cautioning rates are taken from Criminal Statistics England and Wales 1991 and cover police force areas, which do not coincide with CPS branch areas. There will be several branches in each police force area so the figures give no more than a very broad indication of local cautioning practice.

Table 1 shows wide disparity in area cautioning rates, which ranged from 4 per cent to 37 per cent - by coincidence these two extremes were in the same CPS area but different police force areas. There were also very large differences in the degree to which individual police forces approached the CPS for formal pre-process advice, ranging from

HOME OFFICE RESEARCH STUDY No. 137

under one per cent in branches B and F to almost 14 per cent in Branch J. The latter figure was exceptional, in that the national average was 4.3 per cent, and no other branch had an advice file rate of more than 8 per cent. (The branches with the two highest advice rate figures were in the same CPS and police force area.)

Seven out of the 13 branches had termination rates between 10 and 12 per cent, close to the national average of 11.4 per cent. In the event, there was a bias towards areas with above average termination rates, as all the other six ranged from 14 to 20 per cent. When the areas were chosen it had been anticipated that there would be some branches with well below average termination rates since the branches selected included those which at the time were recorded as having the highest and lowest rates in the country. At the time the data for this project were collected, however, these former extremes were both close to the national average.[1] Nevertheless the highest rate within the sample was 20 per cent – double the lowest – so the differences between areas studied remained substantial.

It is difficult to draw any firm conclusions from Table 1 as to the relationship between the termination rate on the one hand and the cautioning and advice rates on the other. Differences in rates between areas were often slight (nine branches had advice file rates within the narrow range of 0.7 to 3.7 per cent), and overall there was no statistically significant relationship between the termination rate and the other variables. However, figures for the branches with the highest and lowest termination rates *did* suggest a possible link with advice and cautioning rates. Branch B, which had the highest termination rate, had the lowest advice rate and was in the area with *much* the lowest cautioning rate. By contrast, Branch J, which had by far the highest advice rate had the equal lowest termination rate. Branch J also had much the highest rate of public interest terminations: the rate for Branch I, from the same police force area, was also well above average (see Appendix B). This may reflect the high level of advice given to the local police. The implication that a high advice rate contributes to a lower termination rate receives tentative support from the finding that there were only four areas with above average advice rates, and they were among the five branches with the lowest proportion of cases discontinued on evidential grounds. It would appear, therefore, that some of the diversity in local CPS practice may be explained by variations in police force policy around the country.

Filtering of cases by the police

Before a file reaches the CPS, the case must go through a number of police filters. The first is the decision whether to arrest the suspect, and thereafter whether to caution, charge or summons them. The police may contact the CPS on an informal or formal basis at the pre-process stage to ask for advice. (For example, what would be the most appropriate charge? Is it in the public interest to proceed?)

---

[1] The CPS reformulatrd their performance indicators in 1991. The quarterly figures published after April 1991 are not strictly comparable with those collected from the services's inception up to that date. This may account for some of the apparent change in the differences between areas between the time the areas were chosenand the time the fieldwork was undertaken.

OVERVIEW

Police in most of the areas studied had some form of central administrative support unit (ASU) to deal with prosecution files. The ASU included both police officers and civilian staff (the proportions and exact roles of each varied between areas). The ASU was usually headed by a Chief Inspector.

It was clear that officers working in the ASUs had become familiar with CPS practices and requirements, and a number of officers in the ASUs felt that as result of their relationship with the CPS a filter had moved back from the prosecutors to the police – they were loath to send cases across to the CPS when they thought termination was the likely outcome. For many, the Code for Crown Prosecutors was seen as a useful source of guidance. In the words of one ASU Chief Inspector:

We're starting to think like lawyers now.

This sifting of cases by the ASU could sometimes have a demotivating effect on front-line officers who felt they had put a lot of work into a case only to see their ASU colleagues apparently siding with the CPS over discontinuance. Those initiating the arrests generally had less direct contact with prosecutors than their ASU colleagues, and often felt more distanced from the CPS perspective. As one officer commented:

The police get divorced from the results of cases – the less control they have, the less they are going to care about the result.

Police officers were asked what criteria they applied when deciding whether to instigate criminal proceedings. The majority of those involved in arresting suspects (typically CID and patrol officers) and those involved in the decision to charge or summons (usually the Custody Sergeant) referred to the Home Office Circular on cautioning (number 59/1990 was the most recent at the time of the study). The ASU officers' role was rather different since they only became involved at a later stage, after the decision to charge or summons had been taken.

The majority of officers with experience of pre-CPS prosecutions thought that the criteria they applied to a case when deciding whether to proceed had changed as a result of the introduction of the CPS, with a decrease both in the number of files submitted for prosecution and in the number of cases going to court. There were mixed views about the desirability of these changes, but acceptance that the separation of roles was irreversible and must be made to work effectively. A separate Home Office project is tracking cases from arrest through to final disposal and will provide more detail about the criteria the police employ when deciding whether to charge or caution suspects (Phillips, C. and Brown, D. forthcoming).

Defendant characteristics

Information was collected on the sex, age, employment status and previous criminal history of the accused for both terminated cases and those where it was decided to prosecute[2].

---

[2] The monitoring forms for terminated cases were filled in by prosecutors involved in the decision to discontinue the case; the control sample forms were completed at a later stage by prosecutors who were not necessarily previously familiar with the case. It was not always possible for all the relevant data to be deducted from the CPS file for this sample. For this reason, any comparisons between the two sets of data in this section – unless otherwise stated – are made only between cases where information was known.

HOME OFFICE RESEARCH STUDY No. 137

Ethnic data was excluded because it could not always be deduced from the CPS files at the time the fieldwork was undertaken. (This has since changed as the CPS, like many other agencies, has extended its range of ethnic monitoring. Data of this kind may in future be used by the Home Secretary to meet the obligations imposed by section 95 of the Criminal Justice Act 1991 whereby information must be published to help those involved in the administration of criminal justice to avoid discriminating against anyone on the grounds of race.)

Table 2 below gives details of the characteristics on which information was collected for both terminated cases and those where there was a conviction on at least one charge. Motoring cases have also been excluded - again the numbers were smaller and, as most were summonses, there tended to be less detailed information on the CPS file.

Table 2
Characteristics for defendants in non-motoring cases[1]

	Terminated cases (N=916)	Cases which resulted in conviction (N=1235)
	%	%
Sex:		
Female	12	14
Male	88	86
Age:		
Under 17	4	5
17-20	24	25
21 to 30	42	44
over 30	31	27
Employment:		
Unemployed	62	59
Employed	28	32
Other	10	9
Known previous convictions	59	58
Defendant charged with more than one offence	22	38
Domestic dispute	13	6
Co-defendants involved	25	21

Notes:
1 Percentages do not always sum to 100 due to rounding

Table 2 shows that there was virtually no difference between the two groups of defendants in terms of sex and very little in respect of age or employment status. A major difference was that terminated cases were less likely than those resulting in conviction to involve multiple offences - the explanation is largely that a single charge dropped will mean complete termination where there is only one charge to begin with, and merely a reduction in the number of counts on the indictment otherwise.

OVERVIEW

Domestic violence cases were relatively more common among terminated cases, reflecting the fact that witnesses' willingness to give evidence can be a problem in such cases - a point confirmed both by the case data and interviews discussed later. It is also notable that domestic disputes made up 16 per cent of cases which the CPS felt should be prosecuted but did not result in a conviction: the outcome in two-thirds of these cases was a bindover.

Previous convictions

For non-motoring cases, there was information showing that the defendant had previous convictions in respect of 59 per cent of terminated cases and 58 per cent of those convicted on at least one offence. For motoring offences the percentages were 18 per cent and 16 per cent respectively. These proportions suggest that the presence of previous convictions has little effect on the likelihood of a case being taken to court – though it is possible that the figures for previous convictions are an underestimate: prosecutors mentioned that sometimes they would only be made aware of a defendant's previous criminal history at court since such details were not always included in the police papers. However, if details were not available from the case papers they presumably could not have influenced the decision as to whether to proceed with the case. (Recent changes, arising from the Working Group on Pre-Trial Issues discussed later, should ensure that information on previous conviction is always provided.)

It is at first sight surprising that an absence of previous convictions was not more strongly related to termination, given that termination in the public interest is less likely to be appropriate for those with previous convictions. Part of the explanation may lie in the fact that some cases were dropped because there were other matters outstanding against the defendant and the penalty was unlikely to be significantly affected by inclusion of additional charges. In three-quarters of these cases the defendant had previous convictions. In addition, provided the case is not serious first offenders are more likely to be filtered out by cautioning. (Absence of previous convictions is one of the criteria to be taken into account when considering whether a caution is appropriate, as set out in Home Office Circular 59/1990.) McConville and Sanders (1992) argued that the CPS should act as a safety net for 'cautionable cases which slip past the police'. It is possible that the CPS may to some extent be fulfilling this function: in cases falling within the terminated sample which were dropped on public interest grounds, and where there were no other matters outstanding, the defendant was less likely to have previous convictions.

Was the initial information sufficient?

For terminated cases, crown prosecutors were asked if they felt there was sufficient information on the initial file to assess whether the case should be dropped on either evidential or public interest grounds. Table 3 shows their responses.

HOME OFFICE RESEARCH STUDY No. 137

Table 3
Adequacy of information on initial file to determine for terminated cases

	Non-motoring cases (N=785)	Motoring cases (N=312)
	%	%
Sufficient evidential and public interest information	74	91
Sufficient evidential information only	4	2
Sufficient public interest information only	11	4
Both evidential and public interest information insufficient	12	3

Table 3 shows that the initial file usually provided sufficient information for the prosecutor to determine whether it was appropriate to proceed with the case but that in more than a quarter of non-motoring cases more information was needed, in terms of available evidence and/or details bearing on public interest. Whilst they were more likely to ask the police for extra particulars where the papers appeared to be lacking in essential detail, prosecutors also contacted the police where the initial file was felt to provide sufficient information for a first review. In over a quarter (28 per cent) of non-motoring offences more information was sought on other grounds - in the words of one prosecutor:

Sometimes it's fairly apparent, but there's an 'i' to dot or a 't' to cross.

Overall, the CPS approached the police for more information in respect of 45 per cent of terminated non-motoring and 25 per cent of terminated motoring cases.

The CPS received information from people other than the police in eight per cent of non-motoring and seven per cent of motoring cases which were terminated. In just over half these cases it was the defence solicitor who volunteered further details. Other possible sources of information included probation officers, social workers and doctors. (The provision of information by non-police sources has been examined in the context of Public Interest Case Assessment projects - see e.g. Stone, 1990; Brown and Crisp, 1992; Inner London Probation Service, 1993.)

Direct contact in this way can give prosecutors access to valuable information which may not be available to them through the police file. Some prosecutors welcomed this contact:

I'm bothered about having the correct version to put before the court.

Although the numbers involved were relatively small, it is of interest that the cases where the CPS were approached directly by a body other than the police were more likely to be dropped on public interest grounds.

OVERVIEW

Working Group on Pre-Trial Issues

The Code for Crown Prosecutors, in addition to defining the evidential and public interest criteria (discussed in Chapter 3) gives a general introduction to the role the Service sees itself playing in the criminal justice process. The Code has been revised several times since the CPS came into operation, to take account of changes in legislation and guidance to criminal justice agencies.

The Working Group on Pre-Trial Issues[3] scrutinised the preparation, processing and submission of files for prosecution. Its report (published in 1990) drew attention to varying pre-trial practices across the country - for example that the content of police files differed considerably from one police force to another. The CPS and police responded by putting together the 'Manual of Guidance for the Preparation, Processing and Submission of Files'. The Manual seeks to standardise the content and format of prosecution files, as well as imposing a timetable for material to be submitted.

The new guidance was introduced nationally in October 1992, shortly after interviews for the present study were completed. A few areas were already introducing the new procedures and some of the comments relating to the consultation process reflected this change. However, the way in which prosecutors exercise their review function has not been changed in any fundamental way by the new guidelines, since these deal with the administrative arrangements and do not bear directly on the criteria set out in the Code.

The Manual defines two categories of file: the abbreviated file and the full file. Both full and abbreviated files include a summary of the evidence including the statement of the victim; a list of witnesses; additional statements from any key witnesses; and details of previous convictions. The full file additionally includes details of *witnesses*' previous convictions and cautions; copies of interview tapes; and original statements from *all* witnesses. A full file must be submitted where there is a charge of assault, where the defendant has pleaded not guilty and/or where a Crown Court trial is a probability. An abbreviated file may be submitted in all other circumstances. Whatever the file category of an individual case, prosecutors may ask the police for further information not included on the Manual's checklist should the need arise. The Manual also provides guidelines for the time that should be allowed for the submission of files and for key stages of the progress of the case.

In most of the areas, prosecutors said that prior to the introduction of the Manual almost all the files they received would now be classified as 'abbreviated', so the additional information in specified cases was seen as a step forward even though (as Table 3 shows) they felt that previously they had generally had enough information to make an initial assessment of cases. One crown prosecutor articulated a recurrent theme, that:

> *the importance to our work of good file presentation just cannot be overstated.*

---

[3] The Group comprised representatives from the Home Office, the Association of Chief Police Officers, Her Majesty's Inspectorate of Constabulary, the Metropolitan Police, the Crown Prosecution Service, the Justices' Clerks' Society and the Lord Chancellor's Department.

HOME OFFICE RESEARCH STUDY No. 137

Prior to the Manual, this was a major source of criticism:

Files are often very disorganised, statements all mixed up and it can be very difficult to extract the essential details.

By contrast, in an area which had adopted the new procedures, the comment was made that:

We were pleased to see guidelines as a means of bringing about tighter supervision – we needed that kind of pressure to improve.

These improvements should by now have been achieved in all areas.

3   Reasons for termination

The creation of the CPS was intended to promote efficiency, consistency, openness and accountability - qualities which the Royal Commission on Criminal Procedure concluded were lacking in the previous prosecutorial arrangements. The Code for Crown Prosecutors was drawn up in order to help prosecutors achieve these objectives. In deciding whether to proceed with a case the strength of the evidence is the first consideration, and only if there is a 'realistic prospect of conviction' will the prosecutor go on to consider whether the public interest will be served by prosecution. If the proper course of action remains unclear after applying these criteria, the Code states that the court should normally be the final arbiter.

On occasions, cases are also dropped for reasons which are largely outside the control of the CPS such as the fact that the defendant cannot be traced, or the court refuses a prosecution request for an adjournment.

Criteria for deciding whether to prosecute

Once the police decide that a suspect should be charged or summonsed, the papers are sent to the CPS who review the file to decide whether to proceed with court action. According to the Code for Crown Prosecutors CPS lawyers should reach this decision by "judicious use of discretion, based on clear principles" rather than "rigid application of the letter of the law".

Evidential criteria

Prosecutors must first examine the quantity and quality of the evidence against a defendant. For example, they need to be satisfied that evidence was collected in accordance with the Police and Criminal Evidence Act (PACE), that admissions or witness statements are reliable, and that any prosecution witness is likely to come up to proof in court. One prosecutor described this aspect of the process as:

> spotting an unexplained gap in the "novel" - if Chapter 1 goes straight into Chapter 3, your warning light goes on: where's Chapter 2?

Public interest criteria

In cases where the prospect of conviction is realistic, the prosecutor must decide whether it is in the public interest to take the matter to court. They must assess the seriousness of the offence, the extent of the defendant's involvement and the willingness of any victim to participate in the prosecution process. The defendant's personal circumstances may also be relevant - a prosecutor may, according to the Code, decide to drop a case where the defendant is either young or elderly, or where they are suffering from a mental disorder.

Overview of reasons for termination

Table 4 summarises the reasons why cases were dropped.

Table 4
Overview of reasons for terminating cases[1]

Reason	Terminated non-motoring (n=359)	Terminated motoring (n=903)
	%	%
Dropped on evidential grounds	58	47
Dropped on public interest grounds	34	24
Defendant not traceable	3	25
Court refused CPS request for adjournment	3	2
Impracticable/impossible to pursue for other reasons[2]	2	2

Notes:
1 Percentages do not always sum to 100 due to rounding.
2 Other reasons include cases where the defendant has died, is confined to a mental hospital etc.

REASONS FOR TERMINATION

Table 4 shows that the majority of non-motoring cases were dropped on evidential grounds, and weaknesses in the evidence also constituted much the most common single reason for termination of motoring cases, accounting for just under half of such terminations. However, overall there was a big difference between motoring and non-motoring cases in reasons for terminations which was mainly caused by difficulties in tracing defendants in motoring cases, where it accounted for almost one-quarter of terminations (the same proportion as public interest criteria). Inability to trace the defendant was not a significant factor for non-motoring cases, where the case is much more likely to be initiated through charge rather than summons.

If the comparison is confined to public interest and evidential reasons (i.e. ignoring those dropped because the defendant was not traceable or for other practical reasons) the difference between the offence categories was much smaller, with 66 per cent of non-motoring and 62 per cent of motoring cases terminated on evidential grounds.

Exceptionally the grounds for termination may be less clear-cut: by far the most common single feature of cases where both evidential and public interest grounds were mentioned (accounting for 39 per cent of such cases) was that the complainant did not wish to continue. If the victim did not want to proceed and would not give evidence, it could be difficult to prosecute, and the public interest in prosecution might also not be clear-cut. In a few instances different criteria were applied to different offences when a case involving more than one offence was dropped. On those occasions when both evidential and public interest criteria were cited the termination has been categorised as evidential in this report in recognition of the fact that this is always the first filter to be applied under the Code.

Cases where a defendant could not be traced

The majority of motoring cases were brought to court by means of a summons: 90 per cent of the terminated sample and 70 per cent of cases where there was a conviction on at least one charge were dealt with in this way. One quarter of defendants summonsed to court on motoring offences had the case against them dropped because they could not be traced. This proportion echoes the findings of a study of disqualified drivers (Mirrlees-Black 1993), which found that many addresses held by the DVLC were incorrect. The proportion of untraceable defendants accused of motoring offences could perhaps be reduced if the police were to seek confirmation of addresses beyond that given on the licence.

Evidence against the defendant

Prosecutors were asked to indicate the broad nature of the case against the defendant in both terminated cases and those where it was decided to prosecute.

HOME OFFICE RESEARCH STUDY No. 137

Non-motoring offences

Table 5 sets out the evidential factors on file for non-motoring cases dropped on evidential and on public interest grounds, and compares these two groups with defendants who were convicted of at least one offence. (Material on file was very different for motoring offences and so these are discussed separately.)

Table 5
Breakdown of evidential factors for non-motoring defendants

Evidential factor	*Case dropped on evidential grounds (n=517)*	*Case not in public interest (n=300)*	*Defendant convicted (n=1,228)*
	%	%	%
Police eyewitness	32	27	36
Victim eyewitness	29	30	34
Independent eyewitness	25	40	45
Full confession	4	35	44
Admission short of a confession	13	14	18
Physical or forensic	26	28	28
Circumstantial evidence	26	10	10
Medical evidence	4	4	6
Information from other suspect	6	2	1
Information from informer	1	1	<1
Distinctive *modus operandi*	1	1	1
Other evidence	2	2	3
No evidence	4	1	<1
Factors per 100 cases	174	196	227

Table 5 shows that cases where the defendant was convicted of at least one offence were more likely to have eyewitness evidence than those where the CPS decided to drop the case - in particular, those dropped on evidential grounds. Termination on evidential grounds was significantly less likely where there was no full confession, and where the case relied partly or wholly on circumstantial evidence.

Motoring offences

As a rule, motoring offences only came to the attention of the CPS because the defendant had witnessed the incident. Eyewitnesses other than the police were occasionally involved - for example, the evidence of victims of other people's careless driving could be relevant. Confessions and admissions also featured much less often in motoring cases, reflecting the fact that evidence is usually clearcut and there is not the same need to seek an admission of guilt from the defendant - for example, a driver either is or is not disqualified, a car either has or does not have a valid MOT etc.

REASONS FOR TERMINATION

Terminations on evidential grounds

Table 6 sets out the reasons given by prosecutors for termination on evidential grounds.

Table 6
Evidential reasons for termination by offence type

Reason	Non-motoring Cases (N=546) %	Motoring Cases (N=174) %
No supporting/corroborating evidence	39	19
Problem with witnesses[1]	35	13
Documents produced	<1	28
No evidence of key element of offence	19	14
Unreliable identification	13	19
Evidence collapsed	8	7
Strong defence	5	5
Evidence weak	4	3
Available evidence improperly obtained or otherwise inadmissible	4	3
CPS/police administrative mistake	1	5
Other	4	6
Number of reasons per 100 cases	132	122

Notes:
[1] "Problem with witnesses" covers the following: conflict between witnesses, witness unreliable or lacking in credibility, witness would probably fail to attend or fail to come up to proof.

It can be seen from Table 6 that lack of supporting or corroborating evidence was the most common reason for dropping cases: lack of evidence of a key element of the alleged offence was also a common reason for dropping a case. Assessments as to the reliability of witnesses, including whether they were likely to attend court, whether they would come up to proof and whether there was conflict between witnesses, also featured strongly in cases dropped. More than a quarter of motoring offences were dropped when the defendant produced relevant documents either at or prior to court.

Weighing the evidence

Whenever the CPS drop a case they are terminating proceedings which the police felt, initially at least, should be taken to court. Some cases which are dropped seem at first to be watertight but the evidence is subsequently undermined, and in some the public interest grounds for stopping the prosecution only emerge at a later stage. However, there are some cases where the CPS decision clearly cannot be reconciled with the police view of the case. Of the 31 police officers interviewed, nearly two-thirds felt that prosecutors (with varying degrees of frequency) dropped cases which they would have 'given a run' and 'got home'.

HOME OFFICE RESEARCH STUDY No. 137

Some officers felt that the reason that many cases were dropped or that charges were reduced was because the CPS 'liked to play it safe', and were therefore prepared to back down too easily. Two examples cited to researchers illustrates this point. In the first, two officers had been called to a domestic disturbance, and both ended up with injuries which meant they had to have substantial time off work. The senior officer had felt that two charges of assaulting a police officer were merited but the prosecutor settled for a bindover, which was described as very demoralising for the injured officers. In the second, a shoplifting case, the officer complained that:

> *The CPS said there was insufficient evidence, despite the fact that it was summer and he was wearing three coats and had a ladyshave in his pocket. The police would have got it home.*

Interviews could, of course, provide only a one-sided view of such cases (and some stories may have been apocryphal), but they are revealing because the views expressed undoubtedly reflected police perceptions in relation to specific cases. However, other cases cast the CPS in a much more positive light. A sergeant now working in an ASU told of a case where he had heard a car alarm go off:

> *I saw these two running away; I thought it was a stonewaller, but the CPS said there wasn't enough evidence. I pressurised them into giving it a spin, and the court dismissed it. They were right, and I'd forced them to do it. After that, I've always looked at their decisions more objectively.*

Terminations on public interest grounds

Table 7 provides a breakdown of the reasons crown prosecutors gave for dropping cases on public interest grounds.

Table 7
Reasons for terminating cases on public interest grounds

Reason	Non-motoring cases (n=311) %	Motoring cases (n=85) %
Nominal penalty likely	29	40
Accused being dealt with for other matters	42	46
Offence trivial	14	27
Complainant did not wish to proceed	16	1
Offence stale	7	25
Defendant mentally ill/stressed[1]	11	8
Youth of defendant	12	1
Defendant of good character/suffered enough	7	4
Recompense made to victim	7	-
Case suitable for caution	4	1
Defendant old/infirm	2	5
Defendant on periphery of offence	2	-
Other	3	8
Reasons per 100 cases	163	167

Note:
[1] The CPS Code has been revised since the study was undertaken and the criterion 'Mental disorder' adopted.

REASONS FOR TERMINATION

Where the offence was discontinued on public interest grounds, the most common reason was that the defendant was being dealt with for other offences - for example, there were other matters outstanding and these offences were taken into consideration, or the individual was already in custody for other offences. In these cases, the additional penalty for the offences in the sample was thought likely to be slight.

The fact that a nominal penalty was likely was mentioned as a factor in just over a quarter of non-motoring cases and well over one-third of motoring cases, though it was only given as the *sole* reason for termination in one-tenth of cases: reasons which helped to explain why a nominal penalty was likely were cited in other cases where the likely penalty was a factor.

In about half of the 17 per cent of cases in which the triviality of the offence was cited, there was overlap with `nominal penalty likely'. Although the triviality of the offence does not appear in the Code as such, it was included as a separate factor at the request of the CPS because it is clearly a valid consideration on the *de minimus non curat lex* principle - 'the law does not concern itself with trifles'. Interpretations of `nominal penalty' seemed to vary by area, and indeed by prosecutor - not all lawyers interviewed felt that cases could properly be dropped just on these grounds:

> *I have never discontinued under likely penalty – I don't see that as my function: if a case is trivial, it shouldn't be prosecuted – you can't just think of the penalty.*

By contrast, another prosecutor commented that:

> *I would be hard pushed to find a case that you could say was trivial - as soon as you do, you are effectively decriminalising.*

Local differences in the prevalence of particular offences, and varying degrees of tolerance of particular behaviour, may also affect how cases are reviewed. One prosecutor working in a provincial town said that he was reluctant to prosecute minor drug offences which he felt would only have resulted in a caution had the offence taken place in a metropolitan area. This view was not one he felt to be echoed by his local force. Other prosecutors had found themselves dealing with cases of civil disobedience, where the object of the defendant's behaviour had been to attract media attention to their cause by means of their court appearance. In such cases, the police may want to see the case dropped but the prosecutor has to assess, in the words of one:

> *How much you are prepared to overlook, and how often they are prepared to commit an offence to get into court and into the national press.*

The police and the CPS need to liaise closely in cases where the police are involved in a local initiative in relation to a particular type of offending (such as kerb-crawling). If the CPS are unaware of such activity, their decisions concerning individual cases may appear to contradict one another. Some prosecutors complained that lack of such background information meant that they were liable to review such cases out of context.

HOME OFFICE RESEARCH STUDY No. 137

The victim's interests

In four-fifths of the cases where the complainant did not want to proceed with the case (16 per cent of non-motoring offences, see Table 7), this was the only reason given for termination: in nearly two-thirds of cases where the complainant changed their mind about going to court, the offence involved a domestic dispute. Often the reason given for the decision was that there had been a reconciliation between the two parties, who were friends or family in any event. Slightly more than half of the cases in which the complainant did not wish to proceed involved violence. More than three-quarters of these were triable either way offences, 13 per cent were summary and 9 per cent were indictable only.

One difficulty in seeking to assess whether a case should be dropped either because the penalty is likely to be nominal or because the offence is considered trivial is that what may seem trivial to the prosecutor may not be viewed in the same light by the victim. Prosecutors frequently mentioned the need to have regard to the victim when assessing public interest, and the need to take account of the victim's interests in reaching a decision whether to prosecute is enshrined in the Victim's Charter (Home Office, 1990).

Occasionally the victim's interests would lead to the case being dropped, for example because the victim was reluctant to give evidence, typically in a domestic case where reconciliation was being attempted. More often, the need to ensure that the victim was satisfied that the matter had been taken seriously, and to enable compensation to be awarded where appropriate, would weigh on the side of continuing with the case:

Some assaults are trivial, but the aggrieved wants his day in court, and compensation.

Recent guidance designed to secure more systematic information about claims for compensation (Home Office Circular No 53/1993) may have a subsidiary benefit in helping the CPS focus on the extent of injury or loss to the victim.

Whether or not compensation was an issue, the impact on the victim was seen as an important factor:

It might seem trivial to the CPS, but not to the victim - only a bar of chocolate, but over time they've lost half their stock; it's only a pedal cycle, but that's their sole means of transport: if the information is available, it might trigger off a thought process which shows it is less trivial.

Cautioning

The prosecution recommended a caution (for which an admission of guilt is required) in only four per cent of the cases terminated on public interest grounds, most commonly because a nominal penalty was likely if the case was taken to court. Other factors mentioned where a caution was recommended included the youth of the defendant (cited

REASONS FOR TERMINATION

in half of the cases), the fact that the defendant was mentally ill or suffering from stress, or that recompense had been made to the victim.

Reasons for termination by offence type

The Code for Crown Prosecutors stresses that each case must be assessed on its own merits but makes it clear that the graver the offence the less likely it is that termination would be in the public interest.

The reason given for termination was examined by types of offence, and substantial differences were found in the degree to which cases were dropped on evidential or public interest grounds.

Non-motoring offences

Table 8 below shows the extent to which the balance between public interest and evidential terminations varies according to the offence category.

Table 8
Overview of reasons for termination for non-motoring offences

Offence	Number of cases	Evidential Grounds	Public Interest	Other
		%	%	%
Shoplifting	77	41	50	9
TWOC/TDA	52	48	42	10
Burglary	84	64	30	6
Other theft	269	62	29	9
Public order offences[1]	65	46	43	11
Criminal damage	96	60	35	5
Other indictable only	33	82	15	3
Other either way	149	66	31	3
Other summary	76	42	42	16
Total	901	58	34	8

Note:
[1] Public order offences include Breach of the Peace.

Table 8 shows that the main distinction between offence category is that public interest criteria were more likely to apply in less serious cases, evidential factors were more common in either way cases (with the exception of shoplifting) and, particularly, indictable only cases. Indictable and either way offences were relatively more likely than summary offences to have been dropped on evidential grounds. This finding is consistent with the view that the public interest is less likely to be served by dropping a case where the charge is serious.

HOME OFFICE RESEARCH STUDY No. 137

Motoring offences

For the most part there were not enough cases within each individual offence category to establish factors associated with the decision not to prosecute. However, cases where the defendant had been asked to produce documents (MOT certificate, insurance details, driving licence etc.) comprised 57 per cent of motoring cases in the terminated sample and just under half of these cases were dropped on evidential grounds (usually where the defendant produced documents at or prior to court) - a further third were dropped because the defendant could not be traced.

Termination rates for different offences

Non-motoring offences

The Home Office produce - for selected offences - information on numbers of cases dropped at committal as well as those withdrawn or discontinued at an earlier stage.

A breakdown of termination rates derived from these data for 1991 is at Appendix C. The figures show fairly small differences in the *overall* termination rates of summary, either way and indictable offences (indeed, they are highest for indictable offences). The main distinction is that the either way cases are more likely to be dropped by the CPS prior to the committal hearing, whereas serious cases are more likely to be filtered out at the committal stage. For example, only eight per cent of robbery cases were filtered out by the CPS compared with 18 per cent of theft and handling. However, 11 per cent of robbery cases but only one per cent of theft and handling cases were dropped at committal, resulting in the same overall attrition rate for robbery and theft.

Motoring offences

A comparison between the offence profile of the terminated sample with that of convicted defendants also indicated that termination rates may vary according to offence type. Only 19 per cent of defendants convicted of motoring offences related to failure to produce documents, whereas such offences formed 57 per cent of those terminated. By contrast, reckless and careless driving cases made up 30 per cent of cases proceeding to court but only 12 per cent of terminated cases. Drink and/or drugs-related driving offences were also less likely than most other motoring offences to be terminated.

Area Breakdown

The extent to which prosecutors terminate cases on evidential and public interest criteria grounds respectively varies between CPS branches. In two branches, 70 per cent of the terminations were on evidential grounds, with around one-fifth terminated on public interest grounds. At the other extreme, fewer than 30 per cent of one branch's terminations were evidential, with over 60 per cent dropped on public interest grounds.

REASONS FOR TERMINATION

(Reasons for termination for each area are summarised in Appendix B.) There were not enough cases to permit a detailed breakdown of reasons for termination having regard to the case profiles of each branch, but on a crude comparison of the cases dropped on evidential or public interest grounds, as set out in Appendix B, there was no significant relationship between the grounds for termination and the overall rate of termination. In other words, there was no evidence that areas with a comparatively high rate of terminations on evidential or public interest grounds respectively necessarily dropped more cases overall.

Reasons why cases were dismissed at court

A sample of 30 not guilty cases was provided from each branch. In 190 of these cases - almost half - evidence had been presented before the case was dismissed. In a quarter of these cases the weakness of the evidence was cited as the reason for dismissal; the strength of the defence accounted for a slightly higher proportion of dismissals. Other reasons why cases were dismissed included (a) an element of doubt; (b) the fact that a key witness failed to attend; and (c) that the witness did not come up to proof. Each of these factors accounted for about 16 per cent of dismissals. As a point of comparison, a study for the Royal Commission on Criminal Justice by Block, Corbett and Peay (1992) concluded that 27 per cent of cases resulting in ordered acquittals at the Crown Court had foreseeable weaknesses, and that a further 28 per cent of acquittals were 'possibly foreseeable'. Although the figures cannot be directly compared, particularly as the offence breakdown and the trial venue were different, the figures in the present study show a broadly similar picture.

Bindovers

Bindovers were seen as having a fairly limited role, but as important nonetheless for certain cases - although the case is discontinued, the threat of further action remains should it prove neceesary:

> *You don't end up with a criminal record, and in many cases it is more effective than a conditional discharge.*

It could also be helpful in domestic cases:

> *If the complainant withdraws at the door of the court, but there's a clear admission – 'she drove me to it' – you need an alternative forum, not the courts.*

Bindovers were most often used in assault cases, including those involving domestic violence.

Elections for Crown Court trial

Although the choice of venue has no direct bearing on the decision as to whether it is appropriate to proceed with a case, it can pose difficulties for the prosecutor.

The Code requires the crown prosecutor to 'weigh the likely penalty with the likely length and cost of proceedings'. However, given that the cost is many times higher at the Crown Court than at a magistrates' court the dilemma is obvious, and this was reflected in interviews:

> *If the defendant elects Crown Court trial, the judge won't like it: it's not worth the time and expense of the Crown Court, but the police don't like it if you drop it.*

Others took the view that where the law allowed a defendant to elect Crown Court trial, it was not for the CPS to intervene:

> *You shouldn't discontinue just because the defendant has elected - the judiciary should deal with the case, and the fact that it went to the Crown Court at the defendant's instigation shouldn't be blamed on the CPS.*

The dilemma posed by the fact that defendants can insist on taking their case to the Crown Court on quite minor matters has been noted in other recent studies (see e.g. Hedderman and Moxon 1991) and prompted the Royal Commission to recommend that the right to jury trial should be curtailed. Whilst that particular proposal has been rejected the present study underlined the problems which the existing arrangements pose in regard to assessment of the public interest.

Sometimes cases originally charged as either way offences can be amended by the CPS to summary only, which results in them being dealt with at a magistrates' court. This was mentioned in a number of police interviews, and there were sometimes misgivings:

> *It's always difficult in assault cases as to what is the appropriate charge. It seems to be the policy of the CPS to prevent cases from going to the Crown Court, and there are times when the extent of injuries make police feel that a more serious charge would be appropriate.*

On the other hand, the opposite situation has been identified as a problem by CPS inspectors:

> *[The inspectors] concluded that a few cases involving minor assaults should have proceeded on lesser charges, which would have been appropriate to the facts; provided the courts with adequate sentencing powers; and resulted in the earlier finalisation of these proceedings. (CPS Annual Report, 1992-1993, p.10.)*

It is clear that quite a difficult balance has to be struck, and this was reflected both in interview and in research which has pointed to extensive alteration of charges in assault cases by the time cases reach court (e.g. Moxon and Hedderman, 1994).

4 Consultation between the police and CPS

Consultation in practice

The Code for Crown Prosecutors states that it should be 'normal practice to consult the police whenever it is proposed to discontinue proceedings instituted by them.'[1] Prosecutors and police were asked about their arrangements for consultation in such situations. Table 9 shows the nature of consultation between the CPS and police.

Table 9
Degree of CPS consultation with the police by case type

Method of consultation	Non-Motoring (n=894) %	Motoring (n=354) %
Orally and in writing	25	15
In writing only	26	27
Orally only	26	18
No consultation	22	42

Table 9 shows clear differences in the pattern of consultation for motoring and non-motoring offences, with no consultation occurring in 22 per cent of non-motoring and 42 per cent of motoring cases. The lack of consultation in so many motoring cases is consistent with the fact that they were often dropped at court when the accused turned up with relevant documents. In non-motoring cases the most common reason for failure to consult was simply lack of time, often because the file had arrived at a late stage. The table masks wide geographical variation in the degree to which there was consultation on the decision not to proceed: in one CPS branch only just over a third of cases were discussed with the police before the case was dropped, whereas in another they were consulted in over 80 per cent of cases.

From discussions with both prosecutors and police it was clear that there was a range of formal and informal mechanisms for consultation on issues relevant to prosecution decisions. Where time allowed, prosecutors said that they would communicate with the police in advance in writing, inviting comments and allowing them time to reply. Others said they included 'action dates' on all correspondence, and that so long as the action dates were realistic, the system usually functioned smoothly. It was felt that officers would respond if they strongly disagreed with the proposed termination:

> *They have an investment in the case and so, one hopes, they have an incentive to get in touch.*

---

[1] In March 1993, following consultation with the police, the CPS implemented a service standard covering the provision to the police of written reasons for discontinuance. The police are sent written notification of proposed discontinuance and are invited to respond, with views on the decision and additional evidence, by a specified date.

27

In cases where there was not enough time to consult in writing prosecutors said that they would discuss the matter over the telephone (generally with an officer in the ASU) and decisions would then usually be confirmed in writing. The decision to drop the case would sometimes be forced on the crown prosecutor at court, for example because a key witness failed to turn up for the hearing, and in such cases prosecutors stressed that they would send a written explanation to the ASU afterwards.

The Manual states that: "Where time permits, the reviewing CPS lawyer should confer with the police before any decision is made to terminate a case". The Code, too, stresses that the CPS should discuss their decisions with the police wherever possible. The timetable which the Manual sets out for provision of files and key stages in the progress of cases should make it easier for the policy on consultation to be implemented in future.

All police officers felt that feedback from the CPS when cases were dropped was valuable, and were concerned that they did not always get it. One ASU Chief Inspector remarked:

> *It's easier when you're not at the sharp end, and I can understand officers' frustrations. There's a lot of resentment by officers who don't understand why the CPS have decided not to prosecute.*

The need for feedback and for better training on the approach which the CPS adopt was underlined by another ASU officer who commented:

> *The police are not aware that the crown prosecutors have written guidelines: they could make the police more aware - they've not sold themselves, so they're thought to be bloody-minded, even though there might be a good reason for their decision.*

There was variation between areas as to the degree and method of consultation between the two agencies. Informal liaison was sometimes helped by having offices in close proximity to each other - for example, the police station generating most of the work for one of the CPS branches was located directly opposite the magistrates' court and prosecutors would often spend time there before court. However, in some areas a strong preference for written consultation was expressed by prosecutors, as it avoided the possibility of later misunderstandings. One particular difficulty is that direct contact between the CPS and the officer most directly involved in a case can be severely hampered by the fact that the police work a shift system and so it can often be difficult or impossible for crown prosecutors to contact them quickly. Perhaps inevitably, the personalities of individuals also influenced the quality of consultation. One officer felt he could approach most of his local prosecutors, but complained that with some:

> *...the attitude comes back "I'm listening to you, but you're wasting your breath"*

An ASU officer was more sanguine:

> *We can always get good feedback on decisions. Even if we don't agree with the outcome we always get a reasoned, written explanation.*

CONSULTATION BETWEEN THE POLICE AND CPS

Most areas had an appeal structure so that cases where there was disagreement on decisions to drop cases could be referred to more senior police and lawyers for consideration, though it appeared the system was rarely used. Various structures were also in place for meetings between the two agencies at management level, and these were often used as an opportunity to discuss policy as well as specific cases. The police had only made the CPS aware that they objected to the decision to drop the case in 2 per cent of the sample. This suggests that whilst police officers often expressed disquiet about terminated cases (and nearly every officer interviewed had several examples readily to hand) either the impact of the problem when it does occur exaggerates its scale, or else the police do not always communicate their disagreement to local prosecutors. The recent implementation by the CPS of a requirement for written explanation of the reasons for discontinuance may alleviate some of these difficulties and improve the level of police understanding of CPS decisions.

Despite the reservations of some officers, based on the view that too many winnable cases were dropped, a majority of police officers accepted the change in the police role which followed from the Prosecution of Offences Act. This acceptance was both at the level of day-to-day processing of cases and at a more abstract level:

At the end of the day, the workload keeps going and you move on to the next one. They're the ones that make the decisions ultimately.

It's better to have an independent system from the police point of view. It's to our advantage not to be judge, jury and executioner.

Advice file cases

As indicated in Table 1, the number of advice cases as a proportion of the total caseload ranged from 0.7 per cent to 13.9 per cent. Advice files provide an indication of the degree of liaison between the CPS and police and, as indicated in Chapter 2, may have some impact on termination rates.

As compared with cases which were terminated or proceeded to court, formal pre-process advice file cases were much more likely to involve juveniles (who comprised 16 per cent of advice cases compared with six per cent of both terminated cases and those proceeding to court). Three-quarters of advice file cases involved defendants with no previous convictions as compared with around one-third of other cases. Advice file cases were much less likely than those which proceeded to court to involve more than one charge (24 per cent as compared with 38 per cent) but were comparable to terminated cases in this respect. Advice was more than twice as likely to be sought in cases involving co-defendants as with cases which proceeded to court.

The kinds of advice sought are set out in Table 10.

HOME OFFICE RESEARCH STUDY No. 137

Table 10
Type of advice sought by the police

Type of advice (n=433)	Non-motoring	Motoring
	%	%
Whether sufficient evidence to charge	84	78
Number/types of charge(s) appropriate	36	47
Whether to caution	18	3
Whether in the public interest to proceed	3	6
Other	6	4
Total requests per 100 cases	147	138

Table 10 shows that concern about the quality of the evidence was much the most common reason for seeking advice, though often it was coupled with a request for advice on the number or type(s) of charge(s) that should be brought, particularly in motoring cases. Advice on whether to caution was rarely sought in motoring cases, but was common with non-motoring offences.

More detailed analysis showed that in 80 per cent of cases where the police asked about the number and types of charges which should be brought, they asked whether there was sufficient evidence to proceed as well. The police asked about evidential sufficiency in 72 per cent of cases where they asked the CPS whether or not the defendant should be cautioned.

The nature of the advice given to the police is set out in Table 11.

Table 11
Advice given to the police

Type of advice	Non-motoring	Motoring
	%	%
No further action	45	31
Proceed on at least one offence	28	38
Proceed on all offences	17	21
Obtain additional evidence	9	11
Formal caution on some/all offences	5	2
Proceed on specimen charges	2	-

Note:
More than one piece of advice could be given, for example to proceed on one offence and obtain additional evidence on others.

Where the police sought advice as to whether or not they should proceed, they were advised to take no further action in 45 per cent of non-motoring cases, and were advised to proceed on one or all offences in an equal number of cases (28 per cent on at least one offence and 17 per cent on all). For motoring cases, they were less likely to advise no further action (31 per cent of cases) whereas they were advised to proceed on one or all offences in 59 per cent of cases.

CONSULTATION BETWEEN THE POLICE AND CPS

Advice to terminate was usually based on lack of evidence on key aspects of the offence, lack of supporting evidence or the unreliability of witnesses. All these factors were even more common in advice file cases than in those that were terminated. However, the high proportion of cases in which no further action was recommended may also have reflected the fact that advice files were particularly common in cases involving juveniles and/or first offenders.

The report of the Working Group on Pre-Trial Issues recommended that two weeks should be allowed for the CPS to provide advice. Bearing in mind that these recommendations had not been implemented at the time of the data collection, in 50 per cent of cases the advice was provided by the CPS within two weeks of receiving the police file and in 82 per cent of cases the advice was provided within one month.

HOME OFFICE RESEARCH STUDY No. 137

5 Timing and notification of decisions to terminate

It is clearly in everyone's interest for cases that are going to be terminated to be dropped as early as possible. Otherwise time spent on preparatory work by both defence and prosecution will be wasted, people will attend court unnecessarily and courts themselves will not always be able to put the time set aside for the hearing to good use. As Table 12 shows, termination in the early stages of the case was comparatively rare.

Table 12
Stage in the proceedings at which cases were terminated

Stage when terminated (n=1260)	Non-motoring	Motoring
	%	%
Before first court appearance	5	5
At first court appearance	7	6
Before subsequent appearance	37	32
At subsequent appearance	51	57
Total	100	100

Table 12 shows that proceedings were discontinued without a court appearance in only five per cent of cases (a figure which the Royal Commission described as "disappointingly small" on the basis of the interim report of the present study) and only slightly more were dropped at the first hearing. It shows, too, that cases were most often terminated at court rather than before the case came to court or between hearings. More detailed analysis of triable-either-way offences showed that 54 per cent were terminated prior to a decision on mode of trial and 46 per cent after.

The Manual of Guidance (which, as indicated earlier, sets out timescales for the provision of files by the police) stipulates that where an abbreviated file is required the time between charge and first court appearance should be four weeks, and where a full file is required five weeks should be allowed. In order to give the CPS sufficient time to review the evidence, an abbreviated file should be prepared within two weeks of charge and a full file within three weeks so that the CPS always has the files two weeks before the court appearance. Although some areas already had local guidelines, the study showed that the time taken was usually well in excess of the requirements which have since been introduced: the police provided the file within two weeks in only seven per cent of cases, and in a further 19 per cent the police provided a file within one month. In sixteen cases the information was received a year or more later.

HOME OFFICE RESEARCH STUDY No. 137

Notification of decisions to terminate

Table 13 gives details of the notification to the defendant of the decision to terminate the case.

Table 13
Notification to defendant of decision to terminate the case (n=1161)

Notification	Non-motoring	Motoring
	%	%
Section 23(3) notice sent at least 48 hours in advance	41	34
Defendant/defence not notified prior to hearing	37	55
Defendant/defence notified informally prior to the hearing	21	10
Section 23(3) notice sent less than 48 hours in advance	1	1
Other	2	-
Total	100	100

Table 13 shows that formal or informal notification prior to the hearing was achieved in 63 per cent of non-motoring and 45 per cent of motoring cases. However, in 37 per cent of non-motoring and 55 per cent of motoring cases there was no advance notification to the defence that the case would be dropped.

The above figures mask substantial differences between areas. The proportion of cases in which notice of discontinuance was sent prior to the first court appearance ranged from less than one per cent to 14 per cent (though the latter figure was exceptional – none of the other branches in the study recorded a figure of more than 7 per cent.) The extent to which a section 23 notice was sent prior to a subsequent court appearance ranged from 16 per cent to 47 per cent between areas.

Reasons for failure to notify defendants of decisions to terminate in advance of the court hearing are given in Table 14.

Table 14
Reasons for not notifying defendants of the decision to terminate

Reasons for lack of advance notification	Non-motoring	Motoring
	%	%
Insufficient time to decide and notify defendant	44	23
Defendant's whereabouts unknown	29	54
Decision made at court	17	14
Defendant in custody	4	4
Offences taken into consideration elsewhere	3	<1
Other	4	4
Total	100	100

TIMING AND NOTIFICATION OF DECISIONS TO TERMINATE

Table 14 shows that lack of time was by far the most common reason given for the failure to notify the defendants in non-motoring cases, accounting for 4 per cent of all such cases, with 29 per cent explained by the fact the defendant's whereabouts were unknown. For motoring cases, the figures were virtually reversed, with whereabouts unknown in 54 per cent and insufficient time accounting for 23 per cent.

Custodial remands

Eighty-seven of those whose case was terminated - just under 7 per cent - spent some time in custody on remand. In the 56 cases where the time on remand was known, in 43 per cent of cases it was a week or less, and in a further 18 per cent it was 1-2 weeks. Thirty-nine per cent of those remanded spent more than two weeks in custody. However, these figures exaggerate the extent to which people were held in custody when the case against them was not considered worth pursuing. This is because in some instances the case was dropped where other more important matters were being pursued, and the defendant was in custody for those other matters.

HOME OFFICE RESEARCH STUDY No. 137

6 Discussion

The available evidence on the prosecution process has in the past been used to support different arguments at different times: in the early years that the CPS was failing to assert its independence sufficiently, later that its assertion of independence was leading to termination of cases which the police felt would have succeeded at court thereby undermining police morale and eroding the fight against crime. The study indicates that there are no simple judgements to be made.

The fact that a higher proportion of proceedings are dropped following the establishment of an independent service should come as no surprise – indeed, it may be taken as evidence that it is fulfilling its function in reviewing cases critically and is consistent with the emphasis on more rigorous case screening which provided much of the rationale for an independent prosecution service. However, if cases were being appropriately filtered out on evidential or public interest grounds it might be expected that fewer cases would result in acquittal and fewer of those convicted would receive a nominal penalty. On the basis of published statistics (e.g. the annual *Judicial Statistics* produced by the Lord Chancellor's Department which show Crown Court acquittal rates and *Criminal Statistics England and Wales* compiled by the Home Office which show sentencing patterns) neither of these things has happened. However, much else has changed and the failure to secure conviction in a higher proportion of cases and the fact that nominal sentences have become more rather than less common cannot be taken as proof of shortcomings in case screening by prosecutors.

Among other developments, the sharp increase in cautioning might have been expected to remove cases that would have resulted in easy convictions (since admitting the offence is a precondition for cautioning). It is reasonable to assume that cautioned offenders, who until recently would have been prosecuted, would have attracted more than their share of nominal sentences, yet the number of discharges has risen. At the level of individual cases the fact that a case is dealt with by way of an absolute or conditional discharge does not necessarily mean that the case should have been dropped: the court will have more detailed information about the defendant, such as that contained in the social enquiry (now pre-sentence) report, that will not have been available to the CPS. A conditional discharge can also be coupled with a compensation order and around one-fifth of compensation orders are imposed with a conditional discharge (see e.g. Moxon, Corkery and Hedderman, 1992). It is apparent from various studies that discharges tend to become more frequent when unemployment rises, and fines become rarer. However, the rise in terminations at a time when sentencing appeared to be becoming more lenient - as judged by both a rise in discharges and a fall in custodial sentences - may have been influenced by the general climate of opinion on criminal justice issues. The recent slight decline in terminations has occurred at a time when use of custody has started to rise again. However, it is too early to say whether the change in termination rates and the changes in sentencing and cautioning have a causal link: this has occurred over a period when the CPS was establishing its identity and refining its policies, and a degree of change would have been almost inevitable through these early years.

The conduct of the investigation does, of course, remain with the police, and while the police could sometimes be critical of CPS decisions to drop cases, crown prosecutors felt that the police did not always respond - or respond adequately - to requests for further investigations. This sometimes resulted in cases being dropped unnecessarily, or meant that the CPS had to proceed with cases with avoidable shortcomings. ASU officers were under no illusions that the police always managed to put their case together well enough:

> *sitting in the middle, you can recognise that it's sometimes down to a lack of evidence or care on the part of the police.*

The Royal Commission on Criminal Justice took on board the fact that the CPS could not require the police to provide additional material and argued for a strengthening of CPS powers to insist on further investigation before a decision in discontinuance is taken (Recommendation 95)

The variation in termination rates between participating areas was somewhat less than anticipated. Part of the explanation may lie in differences in the kinds of cases referred to the local CPS, but interviews did, inevitably, reveal differences in emphasis in interpreting the Code. There was also marked variation between branches in the reasons for termination, with very different ratios of evidential to public interest terminations (as is clear from Appendix B).

The Royal Commission argued that some friction between the police and CPS was inevitable, but they felt it could be reduced through better consultation (Para 5.3). The research reinforces this view: there was no doubt that where consultation was good, this was reflected in a high degree of mutual understanding. However, there did seem to be wide variation. One police officer commented that out of 673 terminations between January and August they only received 54 notices of discontinuance.

By contrast, an officer in another area commented:

> *Cases that are discontinued generally aren't a problem - there's maybe one case in a hundred where we would disagree. But we're always consulted.*

Where police officers expressed dissatisfaction with the decisions made on their cases, this was not necessarily reflected by the ASU in the same force. It is unrealistic to

DISCUSSION

expect crown prosecutors to explain their decisions directly to the front-line officer in the general run of cases - shift patterns alone often preclude direct discussion (although in serious or sensitive cases such discussion is common). The answer appears to lie in better communication within some police forces, so that the ASU always ensures that explanations provided to them are passed on to the officers most directly concerned.

One area went further than most in fostering understanding and cooperation through closer involvement in training:

> We run talks for the police - you get to know people, so you know who is doing the cases – we explain the Code and why we discontinue cases. We emphasise that prosecutors need to keep the police informed, and stress that they are there to be contacted. We have good relationships.

The role of training in improving mutual understanding has been taken on board, in that the CPS has agreed with the police a strategy for CPS involvement in the training of police officers and vice versa. That strategy is being taken forward by a steering group comprising CPS and police representatives.

Some of the difficulties that arise over consultation occur because information is not available early enough to allow for further discussion. The recent Manual of Guidance which specifies both the scope and timing of key stages of the process, should have eased some of the problems identified in the course of the study. It may also have made it easier for the CPS to drop cases earlier, and to implement the Royal Commission's recommendation that:

> Where a case is to be discontinued the CPS should take this decision in time wherever practicable to save the defendant, the victim and the other witnesses from the need to attend court. (Recommendation 96.)

With only one in twenty terminations occurring before the first court appearance there was clearly a long way to go before this goal could be realised. However, a framework for determining when cases should have reached what point is now in place and should help the police and CPS to improve on this performance. As part of these changes, the CPS introduced their own Nartional Operation Practice (NOP) initiative in March 1993, which sets quality of service standards for the work carried out in all its branches. Compliance with the standards does, however, depend in part on the police files being of high, uniform quality throughout the country. As part of the NOP initiative the CPS is monitoring the timing, contents and quality of the files it receives from the police.

Although information was only obtained on proceedings in magistrates' courts, the number of ordered and directed acquittals at the Crown Court (as recorded in *Judicial Statistics*) raise the question whether more cases could have been filtered out at the lower court. Block, Corbett and Peay (op cit) concluded from the research they undertook for the Royal Commission on Criminal Justice that, at a minimum 25 per cent of ordered and directed acquittals in their sample could have been foreseen before, at or just after committal. However, cases often collapse for reasons which the CPS could not have foreseen, or would have had to proceed with even if the collapse of the case was a strong possibility. The Crown Court study for the Royal Commission (Zander and Henderson, 1993) showed that in 20 per cent of the cases where the prosecution offered no evidence a key prosecution witness failed to turn up and in a further 24 per cent the witness(es) did not come up to proof or changed their evidence. Defence submissions, for example on the admissibility of evidence, accounted for 8 per cent of such cases. Other reasons for offering no evidence at the Crown Court covered such matters as medical or psychiatric reports on defendants which suggested it would be inappropriate to proceed; the fact that a co-defendant pleaded guilty or that the defendant himself pleaded guilty to a more serious offence; or the weakness of the case, sometimes exacerbated by poor police work. On occasions the defendant agreed to be bound over and the CPS regarded this as a sensible outcome, for example in a domestic case where the complainant was not keen to proceed. Some of these miscellaneous reasons for termination reinforce the views of the Royal Commission that a crown prosecutor should be able to stop a case at any stage, rather than being compelled to proceed to the Crown Court once commital proceedings were over.

The difficulty which the right to elect, as currently constituted, can pose for crown prosecutors in cases which many would regard as trivial came through repeatedly in interviews. The difficulty of calculating public interest in these circumstances was clearly articulated by Ashworth (1987) not long after the CPS was established:

The law allows a person charged with theft of goods worth £10 to elect Crown Court trial; the cost of that trial, especially if there is a not guilty plea, will inevitably be high in relation to the value of the goods .....so the prosecutor may resolve to drop the case as being insufficiently in the public interest. Yet when defendants and their legal advisers get to know this, they may express their intention to elect Crown Court trial in order to secure impunity.

The interviews confirmed that the ability of defendants to elect in cases which are trivial in relation to the cost of case processing continues to pose a very real dilemma

The variation in the extent to which the police sought advice prior to charge was enormous. The Royal Commission on Criminal Justice called for greater consistency in the way the police seek advice, and advocated guidelines to ensure that the CPS discharged its function under section 3(2) of the Prosecution of Offences Act to advise the police. Changes already in place as a result of the Working Group on Pre-Trial Issues should by now have helped. Despite the difficulty of identifying the influence of any one activity on the criminal process, because of the many interactions in the system, the fact that the growth in terminations has not been rewarded with lower acquittal rates is disconcerting. It could suggest that acquittal rates would remain much the same if fewer cases were weeded out on evidential grounds (in line with past experience) or that

DISCUSSION

recent high profile miscarriages are making magistrates and judges more critical of prosecution evidence. However, any increase in terminations carries a price, both in terms of public perceptions and those of the police.

Public interest terminations raise complex issues. The growing emphasis on the needs of victims and concern that criminals are brought to book is a potential source of tension which may alter the weight which prosecutors have to give to different considerations. Even where the particular circumstances of the case may point to termination, the need to satisfy public expectations (which may not always square with public interest as defined in the Code) may mean that prosecutors have to take a finely balanced decision. The Royal Commission received a considerable amount of correspondence which reflected disquiet about the way cases had been dropped, and observed that:

> *Failure to prosecute in cases that demand that course can do considerable damage to the confidence of the public in the criminal justice system, as many of the letters that we have received testify. (Paragraph 5.28.)*

This anxiety has been taken into account in recent revisions to the Code which are aimed at enhancing public confidence in the prosecution process by strengthening the presumption in favour or prosecution whilst retaining criteria designed to ensure that inappropriate cases are excluded. When the Code was introduced the Director of Public Prosecution said:

> *In cases of any seriousness, there is now clear guidance to Crown Prosecutors that they should usually continue with a case unless public interest factors against prosecution clearly outweigh those in favour. (Mills 1984.)*

The CPS has to operate in an environment in which public opinion, the political climate, the kinds of cases referred to it and the way other criminal justice agencies work can change quickly. The CPS itself, whilst still a relatively young organisation, is experiencing organisational changes as it matures and defines its own role more clearly. The recent revisions to the Code demonstrate that the CPS is responsive to public concerns, and keen to achieve greater consistency than has sometimes been demonstrated in the past. The various recent changes bearing on the prosecution process point to a need for continuing monitoring to ensure that the aims of the Service are being met. The present study will provide part of the baseline against which future performance can be measured.

HOME OFFICE RESEARCH STUDY No. 137

Appendix A

Sample breakdown by area

Branch	Advice cases	Terminated cases	Proceeded to court
A	8	100	170
B	7	93	170
C	41	100	171
D	9	102	170
E	12	99	170
F	27	100	170
G	14	102	164
H	39	100	171
I	75	100	163
J	75	100	164
K	32	116	177
L	74	114	170
M	30	60	171
Total	443	1286	2201

HOME OFFICE RESEARCH STUDY No. 137

Appendix B

Area breakdown of reasons for termination for non-motoring offences

Area		Evidential Grounds	Public Interest Grounds	Other	Overall
		%	%	%	
A	(N=66)	56	27	17	14
B	(N=59)	58	34	8	20
C	(N=64)	58	34	8	15
D	(N=78)	64	35	1	18
E	(N=77)	58	36	5	10
F	(N=64)	59	27	14	12
G	(N=73)	70	22	8	11
H	(N=64)	65	32	3	11
I	(N=67)	49	48	3	16
J	(N=60)	28	63	8	10
K	(N=100)	59	36	5	12
L	(N=89)	70	21	9	15
M	(N=28)	47	46	7	11

Note: [1]Percentages may not sum to exactly 100 due to rounding

HOME OFFICE RESEARCH STUDY No. 137

Appendix C

Rate of termination by offence group

Cases dropped	Indictable only	Either way	Summary non-motoring	Burglary	Robbery	Theft/handling
	%	%	%	%	%	%
Discontinued/withdrawn	8	20	17	17	8	18
Discharged at committed	15	2	<1	2	11	1
All terminated	22	21	17	19	20	19

HOME OFFICE RESEARCH STUDY No. 137

References

Ashworth, A. (1987).**'The "Public Interest" Element in Prosecutions'.** *Criminal Law Review,* **September, 595-607.**

Block, B. Corbett, C. and Peay, J. *(1993) Ordered and directed acquittals in the Crown Court.* **Royal Commission on Criminal Justice, Research Study No. 15**. London: HMSO

Brown, A. J. and Crisp, D. *(1992) 'Diverting cases from prosecution in the public interest. Research Bulletin No 32.* London: Home Office Research and Planning Unit

Crisp, D., Harris, J. and Whittaker, C. *(Forthcoming), Public Interest Case Assessment: evaluation of pilot schemes.*

Crown Prosecution Service *Annual Report* 1992-1993. London: CPS

Crown Prosecution Service (1994). *Code for Crown Prosecutors.* London: CPS

Crown Prosecution Service (1994). *Discontinuance Survey November 1993 - Report.* London: CPS

Gandy, D. (1992). 'Fairness to the CPS' letter to New Law Journal, 188.

Hedderman, C. and Moxon, D. (1991). *Magistrates' court or Crown Court? Mode of trial decisions and sentencing.* Home Office Research Study No. 125. London: HMSO

Home Office (annually). *Criminal Statistics England and Wales. London:* HMSO.

Home Office (1990). *Victim's Charter.* **London:** Home Office.

Inner London Probation Service (1993). *Public Interest Case Assessment: Third annual report of the Inner London Project in Public Interest Case Assessment* 1992-1993. London: ILPS.

Lord Chancellor's Department (annually). *Judicial Statistics.* London: HMSO.

McConville, M., Sanders, A. and Leng, R. (1991). *The Case for the Prosecution.* London: Routledge.

Mirrlees-Black, C. (1992). *Disqualification from driving: an effective penalty?* Research and Planning Unit Paper No. 73. London: Home Office.

Moxon, D. ,Corkery, J.M. ,and Hedderman, C. (1992). *Developments in the use of*

compensation orders in magistrates' courts since October 1988. Home Office Research Study 126. London: HMSO.

Moxon, D. and Hedderman, C. (1994). `*Mode of trial decisions and sentencing differences between courts'.* Howard Journal of Criminal Justice. Vol.33 No2.

Royal Commission on Criminal Procedure (1981). *Report. Cmnd 8092.* London: HMSO.

Royal Commission on Criminal Justice (1993). *Report. Cm 2263.* London: HMSO.

Stone, C. (1990) *Public Interest Case Assessment Volume 2 of the Final Report on the Probation Initiative Diversion from Custody and Prosecution.* Vera Institute of Justice.

Zander, M. and Henderson, P. (1993). *Crown Court Study. Royal Commission on Criminal Justice, Research Study No. 19.* London: HMSO

Publications

The Research and Planning Unit (previously the Research Unit) has been publishing its work since 1955, and a full list of Papers is provided below. These reports are available on request from the Home Office Research and Planning Unit, Information Section, Room 278, 50 Queen Anne's Gate, London SW1H 9AT. Telephone: 071-273 2084 (answerphone).

Reports published in the HORS series are available from HMSO, who will advise as to prices, at the following address: :

HMSO Publications Centre
PO Box 276
London SW8 5DT

Telephone orders: 071-873 9090

General enquiries: 071-873 0011

Titles already published for the Home Office

Studies in the Causes of Delinquency and the Treatment of Offenders (SCDTO)

1. Prediction methods in relation to borstal training. Hermann Mannheim and Leslie T. Wilkins. 1955. viii + 276pp. (11 340051 9)

2. Time spent awaiting trial. Evelyn Gibson. 1960. v + 45pp. (34-368-2).

3. Delinquent generations. Leslie T. Wilkins. 1960. iv + 20pp. (11 340053 5).

4. Murder. Evelyn Gibson and S. Klein. 1961. iv + 44pp. (11 340054 3).

5. Persistent criminals. A study of all offenders liable to preventive detention in 1956. W.H. Hammond and Edna Chayen. 1963. ix + 237pp.(34-368-5).

6. Some statistical and other numerical techniques for classifying individuals. P. McNaughton-Smith. 1965. v + 33pp (34-368-6).

7. Probation research: a preliminary report. Part I. General outline of research. Part II. Study of Middlesex probation area (SOMPA) Steven Folkard, Kate Lyon, Margaret M. Carver and Erica O'Leary. 1966.vi + 58pp. (11 340374 7).

8. Probation research: national study of probation. Trends and regional comparisons in probation (England and Wales). Hugh Barr and Erica O'Leary. 1966. vii + 51pp. (34-368-8).

9. Probation research. A survey of group work in the probation service. Hugh Barr. 1966. vii + 94pp. (34-368-9).

*Out of print

HOME OFFICE RESEARCH STUDY No.137

10. Types of delinquency and home background. A validation study of Hewitt and Jenkins' hypothesis. Elizabeth Field. 1967. vi + 21pp. (34-368-10).

11. Studies of female offenders. No. 1 - Girls of 16-20 years sentenced to borstal or detention centre training in 1963. No. 2 - Women offenders in the Metropolitan Police District in March and April 1957. No. 3 - A description of women in prison on January 1, 1965. Nancy Goodman and Jean Price. 1967. v + 78pp. (34-368-11).

12. The use of the Jesness Inventory on a sample of British probationers. Martin Davies. 1967. iv + 20pp. (34-368-12).

13. The Jesness Inventory: application to approved school boys. Joy Mott. 1969. iv + 27pp. (11 340063 2).

Home Office Research Studies (HORS)

(Nos 1–106 are out of print)

1. Workloads in children's departments. Eleanor Grey. 1969. vi + 75pp. (11 340101 9).

2. Probationers in their social environment. A study of male probationers aged 17-20, together with an analysis of those reconvicted within twelve months. Martin Davies. 1969. vii + 204pp. (11 340102 7).

3. Murder 1957 to 1968. A Home Office Statistical Division report on murder in England and Wales. Evelyn Gibson and S. Klein (with annex by the Scottish Home and Health Department on murder in Scotland). 1969. vi + 94pp. (11 340103 5).

4. Firearms in crime. A Home Office Statistical Division report on indictable offences involving firearms in England and Wales. A. D. Weatherhead and B. M. Robinson. 1970. viii + 39pp. (11 340104 3).

5. Financial penalties and probation. Martin Davies. 1970. vii + 39pp. (11 340105 1).

6. Hostels for probationers. A study of the aims, working and variations in effectiveness of male probation hostels with special reference to the influence of the environment on delinquency. Ian Sinclair. 1971.x + 200pp. (11 340106 X).

7. Prediction methods in criminology - including a prediction study of young men on probation. Frances H. Simon. 1971. xi + 234pp.(11 340107 8).

8. Study of the juvenile liaison scheme in West Ham 1961-65. Marilyn Taylor. 1971. vi + 46pp. (11 340108 6).

9. Explorations in after-care. I - After-care units in London, Liverpool and Manchester. Martin Silberman (Royal London Prisoners' Aid Society) and Brenda Chapman. II - After-care hostels receiving a Home Office grant. Ian Sinclair and David Snow (HORU). III - St. Martin of Tours House, Aryeh Leissner (National Bureau for Co-operation in Child Care). 1971. xi + 140pp. (11 340109 4).

Out of print

PUBLICATIONS

10. A survey of adoption in Great Britain. Eleanor Grey in collaboration with Ronald M. Blunden. 1971. ix + 168pp. (11 340110 8).

11. Thirteen-year-old approved school boys in 1960s. Elizabeth Field, W.H. Hammond and J. Tizard. 1971.ix + 46pp. (11 340111 6).

12. Absconding from approved schools. R. V. G. Clarke and D. N. Martin. 1971. vi + 146pp.(11 340112 4).

13. An experiment in personality assessment of young men remanded in custody. H. Sylvia Anthony. 1972. viii + 79pp. (11 340113 2).

14. Girl offenders aged 17-20 years. I - Statistics relating to girl offenders aged 17-20 years from 1960 to 1970. II - Re-offending by girls released from borstal or detention centre training. III - The problems of girls released from borstal training during their period on after-care. Jean Davies and Nancy Goodman. 1972. v + 77pp. (11 340114 0).

15. The controlled trial in institutional research - paradigm or pitfall for penal evaluators? R. V. G. Clarke and D. B. Cornish. 1972. v + 33pp. (11 340115 9).

16. A survey of fine enforcement. Paul Softley. 1973. v + 65pp. (11 340116 7).

17. An index of social environment - designed for use in social work research. Martin Davies. 1973. vi + 63pp. (11 340117 5).

18. Social enquiry reports and the probation service. Martin Davies and Andrea Knopf. 1973. v + 49pp.(11 340118 3).

19. Depression, psychopathic personality and attempted suicide in a borstal sample. H. Sylvia Anthony.1973. viii + 44pp. (0 11 340119 1).

20. The use of bail and custody by London magistrates' courts before and after the Criminal Justice Act 1967. Frances Simon and Mollie Weatheritt. 1974. vi + 78pp. (0 11 340120 5).

21. Social work in the environment.A study of one aspect of probation practice. Martin Davies, with Margaret Rayfield, Alaster Calder and Tony Fowles. 1974. ix + 151pp. (0 11 340121 3).

22. Social work in prison. An experiment in the use of extended contact with offenders. Margaret Shaw.1974. viii + 154pp. (0 11 340122 1).

23. Delinquency amongst opiate users. Joy Mott and Marilyn Taylor. 1974.vi + 31pp. (0 11 340663 0).

24. IMPACT. Intensive matched probation and after-care treatment. Vol. I - The design of the probation experiment and an interim evaluation. M. S. Folkard, A. J. Fowles, B.C. McWilliams, W. McWilliams, D. D. Smith, D. E. Smith and G. R. Walmsley. 1974. v + 54pp. (0 11 340664 9).

Out of print

HOME OFFICE RESEARCH STUDY No.137

25. The approved school experience. An account of boys' experiences of training under differing regimes of approved schools, with an attempt to evaluate the effectiveness of that training. Anne B. Dunlop. 1974. vii + l24pp. (0 11 340665 7).

26. Absconding from open prisons. Charlotte Banks, Patricia Mayhew and R. J. Sapsford. 1975. viii + 89pp. (0 11 340666 5).

27. Driving while disqualified. Sue Kriefman. 1975. vi + 136pp.(0 11 340667 3).

28. Some male offenders' problems. - Homeless offenders in Liverpool. W. McWilliams. II - Casework with short-term prisoners. Julie Holborn. 1975. x + 147pp. (0 11 340668 1).

29. Community service orders. K. Pease, P. Durkin, I. Earnshaw, D. Payne and J. Thorpe. 1975. viii + 80pp.(0 11 340669 X).

30. Field Wing Bail Hostel: the first nine months. Frances Simon and Sheena Wilson. 1975. viii + 55pp. (0 11 340670 3).

31. Homicide in England and Wales 1967-1971. Evelyn Gibson. 1975. iv + 59pp. (0 11 340753 X).

32. Residential treatment and its effects on delinquency. D. B. Cornish and R. V. G. Clarke. 1975. vi + 74pp. (0 11 340672 X).

33. Further studies of female offenders. Part A: Borstal girls eight years after release. Nancy Goodman, Elizabeth Maloney and Jean Davies. Part B: The sentencing of women at the London Higher Courts. Nancy Goodman, Paul Durkin and Janet Halton. Part C: Girls appearing before a juvenile court. Jean Davies. 1976. vi + 114pp. (0 11 340673 8).

34. Crime as opportunity. P. Mayhew, R. V. G. Clarke, A. Sturman and J. M. Hough. 1976. vii + 36pp.(0 11 340674 6).

35. The effectiveness of sentencing: a review of the literature. S. R. Brody. 1976. v + 89pp.(0 11 340675 4).

36. IMPACT. Intensive matched probation and after-care treatment. Vol. II - The results of the experiment. M. S. Folkard, D. E. Smith and D. D. 1976. xi + 40pp. (0 11 340676 2).

37. Police cautioning in England and Wales. J. A. Ditchfield. 1976. v + 31pp. (0 11 340677 0).

38. Parole in England and Wales. C. P. Nuttall, with E. E. Barnard, A. J. Fowles, A. Frost, W. H. Hammond, P. Mayhew, K. Pease, R. Tarling and M. J. Weatheritt. 1977. vi + 90pp. (0 11 340678 9).

39. Community service assessed in 1976. K. Pease, S. Billingham and I. Earnshaw. 1977. vi + 29pp. (0 11 340679 7).

Out of print

PUBLICATIONS

40. Screen violence and film censorship: a review of research. Stephen Brody. 1977. vii + 179pp. (0 11 340680 0).

41. Absconding from borstals. Gloria K. Laycock. 1977. v + 82pp. (0 11 340681 9).

42. Gambling: a review of the literature and its implications for policy and research. D. B. Cornish. 1978. xii + 284pp. (0 11 340682 7).

43. Compensation orders in magistrates' courts. Paul Softley. 1978. v + 41pp. (0 11 340683 5).

44. Research in criminal justice. John Croft. 1978. iv + 16pp. (0 11 340684 3).

45. Prison welfare: an account of an experiment at Liverpool. A. J. Fowles. 1978. v + 34pp. (0 11 340685 1).

46. Fines in magistrates' courts. Paul Softley. 1978. v + 42pp. (0 11 340686 X).

47. Tackling vandalism. R. V. G Clarke (editor), F. J. Gladstone, A. Sturman and Sheena Wilson 1978. vi + 91pp. (0 11 340687 8).

48. Social inquiry reports: a survey. Jennifer Thorpe. 1979. vi + 55pp. (0 11 340688 6).

49. Crime in public view. P. Mayhew, R. V. G. Clarke, J. N. Burrows, J. M. Hough and S. W. C. Winchester. 1979. v + 36pp. (0 11 340689 4).

50. Crime and the community. John Croft. 1979. v + 16pp. (0 11 340690 8).

51. Life-sentence prisoners. David Smith (editor), Christopher Brown, Joan Worth, Roger Sapsford and Charlotte Banks (contributors). 1979. iv + 51pp. (0 11 340691 6).

52. Hostels for offenders. Jane E. Andrews, with an appendix by Bill Sheppard. 1979. v + 30pp. (0 11 340692 4).

53. Previous convictions, sentence and reconviction: a statistical study of a sample of 5,000 offenders convicted in January 1971. G. J. O. Phillpotts and L. B. Lancucki. 1979. v + 55pp. (0 11 340693 2).

54. Sexual offences, consent and sentencing. Roy Walmsley and Karen White. 1979. vi + 77pp. (0 11 340694 0).

55. Crime prevention and the police. John Burrows, Paul Ekblom and Kevin Heal. 1979. v + 37pp. (0 11 340695 9).

56. Sentencing practice in magistrates' courts. Roger Tarling, with the assistance of Mollie Weatheritt. 1979. vii + 54pp. (0 11 340696 7).

57. Crime and comparative research. John Croft. 1979. iv + 16pp. (0 11 340697 5).

58. Race, crime and arrests. Philip Stevens and Carole F. Willis. 1979. v + 69pp. (0 11 340698 3).

HOME OFFICE RESEARCH STUDY No.137

59. Research and criminal policy. John Croft. 1980. iv + 14pp. (0 11 340699 1).
60. Junior attendance centres. Anne B. Dunlop. 1980. v + 47pp. (0 11 340700 9).
61. Police interrogation: an observational study in four police stations. Paul Softley, with the assistance of David Brown, Bob Forde, George Mair and David Moxon. 1980. vii + 67pp. (0 11 340701 7).
62. Co-ordinating crime prevention efforts. F. J. Gladstone. 1980. v + 74pp. (0 11 340702 5).
63. Crime prevention publicity: an assessment. D. Riley and P. Mayhew. 1980. v + 47pp.(0 11 340703 3).
64. Taking offenders out of circulation. Stephen Brody and Roger Tarling. 1980. v + 46pp.(0 11 340704 1).
65. Alcoholism and social policy: are we on the right lines? Mary Tuck. 1980. v + 30pp. (0 11 340705 X).
66. Persistent petty offenders. Suzan Fairhead. 1981. vi + 78pp. (0 11 340706 8).
67. Crime control and the police. Pauline Morris and Kevin Heal. 1981. v + 71pp. (0 11 340707 6).
68. Ethnic minorities in Britain: a study of trends in their position since 1961. Simon Field, George Mair, Tom Rees and Philip Stevens. 1981. v + 48pp. (0 11 340708 4).
69. Managing criminological research. John Croft. 1981. iv + 17pp. (0 11 340709 2).
70. Ethnic minorities, crime and policing: a survey of the experiences of West Indians and whites. Mary Tuck and Peter Southgate. 1981. iv + 54pp. (0 11 340765 3).
71. Contested trials in magistrates' courts. Julie Vennard. 1982. v + 32pp. (0 11 340766 1).
72 Public disorder: a review of research and a study in one inner city area. Simon Field and Peter Southgate. 1982. v + 77pp. (0 11 340767 X).
73. Clearing up crime. John Burrows and Roger Tarling. 1982. vii + 31pp. (0 11 340768 8).
74. Residential burglary: the limits of prevention. Stuart Winchester and Hilary Jackson. 1982. v + 47pp. (0 11 340769 6).
75. Concerning crime. John Croft. 1982. iv + 16pp. (0 11 340770 X).
76. The British Crime Survey: first report. Mike Hough and Pat Mayhew. 1983. v + 62pp. (0 11 340786 6).
77. Contacts between police and public: findings from the British Crime Survey. Peter Southgate and Paul Ekblom. 1984. v + 42pp. (0 11 340771 8).

Out of print

PUBLICATIONS

78. Fear of crime in England and Wales. Michael Maxfield. 1984. v + 57pp. (0 11 340772 6).

79. Crime and police effectiveness. Ronald V Clarke and Mike Hough 1984. iv + 33pp. (0 11 340773 3).

80. The attitudes of ethnic minorities. Simon Field. 1984. v + 49pp. (0 11 340774 2).

81. Victims of crime: the dimensions of risk. Michael Gottfredson. 1984. v + 54pp. (0 11 340775 0).

82. The tape recording of police interviews with suspects: an interim report. Carole Willis. 1984. v + 45pp. (0 11 340776 9).

83. Parental supervision and juvenile delinquency. David Riley and Margaret Shaw. 1985. v + 90pp. (0 11 340799 8).

84. Adult prisons and prisoners in England and Wales 1970-1982: a review of the findings of social research. Joy Mott. 1985. vi + 73pp. (0 11 340801 3).

85. Taking account of crime: key findings from the 1984 British Crime Survey. Mike Hough and Pat Mayhew. 1985. vi + 115pp. (0 11 341810 2).

86. Implementing crime prevention measures. Tim Hope. 1985. vi + 82pp. (0 11 340812 9).

87. Resettling refugees: the lessons of research. Simon Field. 1985. vi + 66pp. (0 11 340815 3).

88. Investigating burglary: the measurement of police performance. John Burrows. 1986. vi + 36pp.(0 11 340824 2)

89. Personal violence. Roy Walmsley. 1986. vi + 87pp. (0 11 340827 7).

90. Police-public encounters. Peter Southgate. 1986. vi + 150pp. (0 11 340834 X).

91. Grievance procedures in prisons. John Ditchfield and Claire Austin. 1986. vi + 87pp. (0 11 340839 0).

92. The effectiveness of the Forensic Science Service. Malcolm Ramsay. 1987. v + 100pp. (0 11 340842 0).

93. The police complaints procedure: a survey of complainant's views. David Brown. 1987. v + 98pp. (0 11 340853 6).

94. The validity of the reconviction prediction score. Denis Ward. 1987. vi + 46. (0 11 340882 X).

95. Economic aspects of the illicit drug market enforcement policies in the United Kingdom. Adam Wagstaff and Alan Maynard. 1988. vii + 156pp. (0 11 340883 8)

96. Schools, disruptive behaviour and deliquency: a review of literature. John Graham. 1988. v + 70pp. (0 11 340887 0).

97. The tape recording of police interviews with suspects: a second interim report. Carole Willis, John Macleod and Peter Naish. 1988. vii + 97pp. (011 340890 0).

Out of print

HOME OFFICE RESEARCH STUDY No.137

98. Triable-either-way cases: Crown Court or magistrate's court. David Riley and Julie Vennard. 1988. v + 52pp. (0 11 340891 9).

99. Directing patrol work: a study of uniformed policing. John Burrows and Helen Lewis. 1988 v + 66pp. (0 11 340891 9)

100. Probation day centres. George Mair. 1988. v + 44pp. (0 11 340894 3).

101. Amusement machines: dependency and delinquency. John Graham. 1988. v + 48pp. (0 11 340895 1).

102. The use and enforcement of compensation orders in magistrates' courts. Tim Newburn. 1988. v + 49pp. (0 11 340 896 X)

103. Sentencing practice in the Crown Court. David Moxon. 1988. v + 90pp. (0 11 340902 8).

104. Detention at the police station under the Police and Criminal Evidence Act 1984. David Brown. 1988. v + 88pp. (0 11340908 7).

105. Changes in rape offences and sentencing. Charles Lloyd and Roy Walmsley. 1989. vi + 53pp. (0 11 340910 9).

106. Concerns about rape. Lorna Smith. 1989. v + 48pp. (0 11 340911 7).

107. Domestic violence. Lorna Smith. 1989. v + 132pp. (0 11 340925 7)

108. Drinking and disorder: a study of non-metropolitan violence. Mary Tuck. 1989. v + 111pp. (011 340926 5).

109. Special security units. Roy Walmsley. 1989. v + 114pp. (0 11 340961 3).

110. Pre-trial delay: the implications of time limits. Patricia Morgan and Julie Vennard. 1989. v + 66pp. (0 11 340964 8).

111. The 1988 British Crime Survey. Pat Mayhew, David Elliott and Lizanne Dowds. 1989. v + 133pp. (0 11 340965 6).

112. The settlement of claims at the Criminal Injuries Compensation Board. Tim Newburn. 1989. v + 40pp. (0 11 340967 2)

113. Race, community groups and service delivery. Hilary Jackson and Simon Field. 1989. v + 62pp.(0 11 340972 9)

114. Money payment supervision orders: probation policy and practice. George Mair and Charles Lloyd. 1989.v + 40pp. (0 11 340971 0).

115. Suicide and self-injury in prison: a literature review. Charles Lloyd. 1990. v + 69pp. (0 11 3409745 5).

116. Keeping in Touch: police-victim communication in two areas. Tim Newburn and Susan Merry. 1990. v + 52pp. (0 11 340974 5).

Out of print

PUBLICATIONS

117. The police and public in England and Wales: a British Crime Survey report. Wesley G. Skogan. 1990. vi + 74pp. (0 11 340995 8).

118. Control in prisons: a review of the literature. John Ditchfield. 1990 (0 11 340996 6).

119. Trends in crime and their interpretation: a study of recorded crime in post-war England and Wales. Simon Field. 1990. (0 11 340994 X).

120. Electronic monitoring: the trials and their results. George Mair and Claire Nee. 1990. v + 79pp (0 11 340998 2).

121. Drink driving: the effects of enforcement. David Riley. 1991. viii + 78pp (0 11 340999 0).

122. Managing difficult prisoners: the Parkhurst Special Unit. Roy Walmsley (Ed.) 1991. x + 139pp (0 11 341008 5).

123. Investigating burglary: the effects of PACE. David Brown. 1991. xii + 106pp. (0 11 341011 5).

124. Traffic policing in changing times. Peter Southgate and Catriona Mirrlees-Black. 1991. viii + 139pp (0 11 341019 0)

125. Magistrates' court or Crown Court ? Mode of trial decisions and sentencing. Carol Hedderman and David Moxon. 1992. vii + 53pp. (0 11 341036 0).

126. Developments in the use of compensation orders in magistrates' courts since October 1988. David Moxon, John Martin Corkery and Carol Hedderman. 1992. x + 48pp. (0 11 341042 5).

127. A comparative study of firefighting arrangements in Britain, Denmark, the Netherlands and Sweden. John Graham, Simon Field, Roger Tarling and Heather Wilkinson. 1992. x + 57pp. (0 11 341043 3).

128. The National Prison Survey 1991: main findings. Roy Walmsley, Liz Howard and Sheila White. 1992. xiv + 82pp. (0 11 341051 4).

129. Changing the Code: police detention under the revised PACE Codes of Practice. David Brown, Tom Ellis and Karen Larcombe. 1992. viii + 122pp. (0 11 341052 2).

130. Car theft: the offender's perspective. Roy Light, Claire Nee and Helen Ingham. 1993. x + 89pp. (0 11 341069 7).

131. Housing, Community and Crime: The Impact of the Priority Estates Project. Janet Foster and Timothy Hope with assistance from Lizanne Dowds and Mike Sutton. 1993. xi + 118. (0 11 341078 6).

132. The 1992 British Crime Survey. Pat Mayhew, Natalie Aye Maung and Catriona Mirrlees-Black. 1993. xiii + 206. (0 11 341094 8).

Out of print

HOME OFFICE RESEARCH STUDY No.137

Research and Planning Unit Papers (RPUP)

1. Uniformed police work and management technology. J. M. Hough. 1980.
2. Supplementary information on sexual offences and sentencing. Roy Walmsley and Karen White. 1980.
3. Board of visitor adjudications. David Smith, Claire Austin and John Ditchfield. 1981.
4. Day centres and probation. Suzan Fairhead, with the assistance of J.Wilkinson-Grey. 1981.
5. Ethnic minorities and complaints against the police. Philip Stevens and Carole Willis. 1982.
6. Crime and public housing. Mike Hough and Pat Mayhew (editors). 1982.
7. Abstracts of race relations research. George Mair and Philip Stevens (editors). 1982.
8. Police probationer training in race relations. Peter Southgate. 1982.
9. The police response to calls from the public. Paul Ekblom and Kevin Heal. 1982.
10. City centre crime: a situational approach to prevention. Malcolm Ramsay. 1982.
11. Burglary in schools: the prospects for prevention. Tim Hope. 1982.
12. Fine enforcement. Paul Softley and David Moxon. 1982.
13. Vietnamese refugees. Peter Jones. 1982.
14. Community resources for victims of crime. Karen Williams. 1983.
15. The use, effectiveness and impact of police stop and search powers. Carole Willis. 1983.
16. Acquittal rates. Sid Butler. 1983.
17. Criminal justice comparisons: the case of Scotland and England and Wales. Lorna J. F. Smith. 1983.
18. Time taken to deal with juveniles under criminal proceedings. Catherine Frankenburg and Roger Tarling. 1983.
19. Civilian review of complaints against the police: a survey of the United States literature. David C. Brown. 1983.
20. Police action on motoring offences. David Riley. 1983.
21. Diverting drunks from the criminal justice system. Sue Kingsley and George Mair. 1983.
22. The staff resource implications of an independent prosecution system. Peter R. Jones. 1983.

---

*Out of print

PUBLICATIONS

23. Reducing the prison population: an exploratory study in Hampshire. David Smith, Bill Sheppard, George Mair, Karen Williams. 1984.

24. Criminal justice system model: magistrates' courts sub-model. Susan Rice. 1984.

25. Measures of police effectiveness and efficiency. Ian Sinclair and Clive Miller. 1984.

26. Punishment practice by prison Boards of Visitors. Susan Iles, Adrienne Connors, Chris May, Joy Mott. 1984.

27. Reparation, conciliation and mediation: current projects and plans in England and Wales. Tony Marshall. 1984.

28. Magistrates' domestic courts: new perspectives. Tony Marshall (editor). 1984.

29. Racism awareness training for the police. Peter Southgate. 1984.

30. Community constables: a study of a policing initiative. David Brown and Susan Iles. 1985.

31. Recruiting volunteers. Hilary Jackson. 1985.

32. Juvenile sentencing: is there a tariff? David Moxon, Peter Jones, Roger Tarling. 1985.

33. Bringing people together: mediation and reparation projects in Great Britain. Tony Marshall and Martin Walpole. 1985.

34. Remands in the absence of the accused. Chris May. 1985.

35. Modelling the criminal justice system. Patricia M Morgan. 1985.

36. The criminal justice system model: the flow model. Hugh Pullinger. 1986.

37. Burglary: police actions and victim views. John Burrows. 1986.

38. Unlocking community resources: four experimental government small grants schemes. Hilary Jackson. 1986.

39. The cost of discriminating: a review of the literature. Shirley Dex. 1986.

40. Waiting for Crown Court trial: the remand population. Rachel Pearce. 1987.

41. Children's evidence: the need for corroboration. Carol Hedderman. 1987.

42. A prelimary study of victim offender mediation and reparation schemes in England and Wales. Gwynn Davis, Jacky Boucherat, David Watson, Adrian Thatcher (Consultant). 1987.

43. Explaining fear of crime: evidence from the 1984 British Crime Survey. Michael Maxfield. 1987.

44. Judgements of crime seriousness: evidence from the 1984 British Crime Survey. Ken Pease. 1988.

---

*Out of print

HOME OFFICE RESEARCH STUDY No.137

45. Waiting time on the day in magistrates' courts: a review of case listings practises. David Moxon and Roger Tarling (editors). 1988.

46. Bail and probation work: the ILPS temporary bail action project. George Mair. 1988.

47. Police work and manpower allocation. Roger Tarling. 1988.

48. Computers in the courtroom. Carol Hedderman. 1988.

49. Data interchange between magistrates' courts and other agencies. Carol Hedderman. 1988.

50. Bail and probation work II: the use of London probation/bail hostels for bailees. Helen Lewis and George Mair. 1989.

51. The role and function of police community liaison officers. Susan V Phillips and Raymond Cochrane. 1989.

52. Insuring against burglary losses. Helen Lewis. 1989.

53. Remand decisions in Brighton and Bournemouth. Patricia Morgan and Rachel Pearce. 1989.

54. Racially motivated incidents reported to the police. Jayne Seagrave. 1989.

55. Review of research on re-offending of mentally disordered offenders. David J. Murray. 1990.

56. Risk prediction and probation: papers from a Research and Planning Unit workshop. George Mair (editor). 1990.

57. Household fires: findings from the British Crime Survey 1988. Chris May. 1990.

58. Home Office funding of victim support schemes - money well spent? Justin Russell. 1990.

59. Unit fines: experiments in four courts. David Moxon, Mike Sutton and Carol Hedderman. 1990.

60. Deductions from benefit for fine default. David Moxon, Carol Hedderman and Mike Sutton. 1990.

61. Monitoring time limits on custodial remands. Paul F. Henderson. 1991.

62. Remands in custody for up to 28 days: the experiments. Paul F. Henderson and Patricia Morgan. 1991.

63. Parenthood training for young offenders: an evaluation of courses in Young Offender Institutions. Diane Caddle. 1991.

64. The multi-agency approach in practice: the North Plaistow racial harassment project. William Saulsbury and Benjamin Bowling. 1991.

Out of print

PUBLICATIONS

65. Offending while on bail: a survey of recent studies. Patricia M. Morgan. 1992.

66. Juveniles sentenced for serious offences: a comparison of regimes in Young Offender Institutions and Local Authority Community Homes. John Ditchfield and Liza Catan. 1992.

67. The management and deployment of police armed response vehicles. Peter Southgate. 1992.

68. Using psychometric personality tests in the selection of firearms officers. Catriona Mirrlees-Black. 1992.

69. Bail information schemes: practice and effect. Charles Lloyd. 1992.

70. Crack and cocaine in England and Wales. Joy Mott (editor). 1992

71. Rape: from recording to conviction. Sharon Grace, Charles Lloyd and Lorna J.F. Smith. 1992.

72. The National Probation Survey 1990. Chris May. 1993.

73. Public satisfaction with police services. Peter Southgate and Debbie Crisp. 1993.

74. Disqualification from driving: an effective penalty?. Catriona Mirrlees-Black. 1993.

75. Detention under the Prevention of Terrorism (Temporary Provisions) Act 1989: Access to legal advice and outside contact. David Brown. 1993.

76. Panel assessment schemes for mentally disordered offenders. Carol Hedderman. 1993.

77. Cash-limiting the probation service: a case study in resource allocation. Simon Field and Mike Hough. 1993.

78. The probation response to drug misuse. Claire Nee and Rae Sibbitt. 1993.

79. Approval of rifle and target shooting clubs: the effects of the new and revised criteria. John Martin Corkery. 1993.

80. The long-term needs of victims: A review of the literature. Tim Newburn. 1993.

81. The welfare needs of unconvicted prisoners. Diane Caddle and Sheila White. 1994.

82. Racially motivated crime: a British Crime Survey analysis. Natalie Aye Maung and Catriona Mirrlees-Black. 1994.

83. Mathematical models for forecasting Passport demand. Andy Jones and John MacLeod. 1994.

84. The theft of firearms. John Corkery. 1994.

85. Equal opportunities and the Fire Service. Tom Bucke. 1994.

Out of print

HOME OFFICE RESEARCH STUDY No.137

Research Findings

(These are summaries of reports and are also available from the Information Section)

1. Magistrates' court or Crown Court? Mode of trial decisions and their impact on sentencing. Carol Hedderman and David Moxon. 1992.
2. Surveying crime: findings from the 1992 British Crime Survey. Pat Mayhew and Natalie Aye Maung. 1992.
3. Car Theft: the offenders's perspective: Claire Nee. 1993.
4. The National Prison survey 1991: main findings. Roy Walmsley, Liz Howard and Sheila White. 1993.
5. Changing the Code: Police detention under the revised PACE codes of practice. David Brown, Tom Ellis and Karen Larcombe. 1993.
6. Rifle and pistol target shooting clubs: The effects of new approval criteria. John M Corkery. 1993.
7. Self-reported drug misuse in England and Wales. Main findings from the 1992 British Crime Survey. Joy Mott and Catriona Mirrlees-Black. 1993.
8. Findings from the International Crime Survey. Pat Mayhew. 1994.
9. Fear of Crime: Findings from the 1992 British Crime Survey. Catriona Mirrlees-Black and Natalie Aye Maung. 1994.
10. Does the Criminal Justice system treat men and women differently? Carol Hedderman and Mike Hough. 1994.
11. Participation in Neighbourhood Watch: Findings from the 1992 British Crime Survey. Lizanne Dowds and Pat Mayhew. 1994.
12. Not published yet.
13. Equal opportunities and the Fire Service. Tom Bucke. 1994.
14. Trends in Crime: Findings from the 1994 British Crime Survey. Pat Mayhew, Catriona Mirrlees-Black and Natalie Aye Maung. 1994.

Research Bulletin (available from the Information Section)

The Research Bulletin is published twice a year and consists mainly of short articles relating to projects which are part of the Home Office Research and Planning Unit's research programme.

*Out of print

PUBLICATIONS

Occasional Papers

(These can be purchased from the main Home Office Library Publications Unit, 50 Queen Anne's Gate, London SWIH 9AT. Telephone 071-273 2302 for information on price and availability. Those marked with an asterisk are out of print.)

*The 'watchdog' role of Boards of Visitors. Mike Maguire and Jon Vagg. 1984.

Shared working between Prison and Probation Officers. Norman Jepson and Kenneth Elliot. 1985.

After-care Services for Released Prisoners: A Review of the Literature. Kevin Haines. 1990.

*Arts in Prisons: towards a sense of achievement. Anne Peaker and Jill Vincent. 1990.

Pornography: impacts and influences. Dennis Howitt and Guy Cumberbatch. 1990.

*An evaluation of the live link for child witnesses. Graham Davies and Elizabeth Noon. 1991.

Mentally disordered prisoners. John Gunn, Tony Maden and Mark Swinton. 1991.

Coping with a crisis: the introduction of three and two in a cell. T G Weiler. 1992.

Psychiatric Assessment at the Magistrates' Court. Philip Joseph. 1992.

Measurement of caseload weightings in magistrates' courts. Richard J Gadsden and Graham J Worsdale. 1992.

The CDE of scheduling in magistrates' courts. John W Raine and Michael J Willson. 1992.

Employment opportunities for offenders. David Downes. 1993.

Sex offenders: a framework for the evaluation of community-based treatment. Mary Barker and Rod Morgan. 1993.

Suicide attempts and self-injury in male prisons. Alison Liebling and Helen Krarup. 1993.

Measurement of caseload weightings associated with the Children's Act. Richard J Gadsden and Graham J Worsdale. 1994. (available from the RPU Information Section).

Managing difficult prisoners: The Lincoln and Hull special units.

Professor Keith Bottomley, Professor Norman Jepson, Mr Kenneth Elliott and Dr Jeremy Coid. 1994 (available from RPU Information Section).

The Nacro diversion iniative for mentally disturbed offenders: an account and an evaluation. Home Office, NACRO and Mental Health Foundation (available from Information Section).

Out of print

HOME OFFICE RESEARCH STUDY No.137

Other Publications by members of RPU (available from HMSO)

Designing out crime. R. V. G. Clarke and P. Mayhew (editors). 1980. viii + 186pp. (0 11 340732 7).

Policing today. Kevin Heal, Roger Tarling and John Burrows (editors). v + 181pp. (0 11 340800 5).

Managing criminal justice: a collection of papers. David Moxon (editor). 1985. vi + 222pp. (0 11 340811 0).

Situational crime prevention: from theory into practice. Kevin Heal and Gloria Laycock (editors). 1986. vii + 166pp. (0 11 340826 9)

Communities and crime reduction. Tim Hope and Margaret Shaw (editors). 1988. vii + 311pp. (11 340892 7).

New directions in police training. Peter Southgate (editor). 1988. xi + 256pp (11 340889 7).

Crime and Accountability: Victim/Offender Mediation in Practice. Tony F Marshall and Susan Merry. 1990. xii + 262. (0 11 340973 7).

Community Work and the Probation Service. Paul Henderson and Sarah del Tufo. 1991. vi + 120. (0 11 341004 2).

Part Time Punishment? George Mair. 1991. 258 pp. (0 11 340981 8).

Analysing Offending Data, Models and Interpretations. Roger Tarling. 1993. viii + 203. (0 11 341080 8).

Out of print